Communication, Language and Literacy from Birth to Five

Avril Brock and Carolynn Rankin

ANDOVER COLLEGE

$\oint$SAGE

Los Angeles • London • New Delhi • Singapore

© Avril Brock and Carolynn Rankin 2008

Chapter 4 © SAGE, 2008

First published 2008

Apart from any fair dealing for the purposes of research or private study, or criticism or review, as permitted under the Copyright, Designs and Patents Act, 1988, this publication may be reproduced, stored or transmitted in any form, or by any means, only with the prior permission in writing of the publishers, or in the case of reprographic reproduction, in accordance with the terms of licences issued by the Copyright Licensing Agency. Enquiries concerning reproduction outside those terms should be sent to the publishers.

SAGE Publications Ltd
1 Oliver's Yard
55 City Road
London EC1Y 1SP

SAGE Publications Inc
2455 Teller Road
Thousand Oaks, California 91320

SAGE Publications India Pvt Ltd
B-1/I1 Mohan Cooperative Industrial Area
Mathura Road
New Delhi 110 044

SAGE Publications Asia-Pacific Pte Ltd
33 Pekin Street # 02–01
Far East Square
Singapore 048763

Library of Congress Control Number: 2007938622

British Library Cataloguing in Publication Data
A catalogue record for this book is available from the British Library

ISBN-978-1-4129-4589-9
ISBN-978-1-4129-4950-5 (pbk)

Typeset by Pantek Arts Ltd, Maidstone, Kent
Printed in Great Britain by Cromwell Press Ltd, Trowbridge, Wiltshire
Printed on paper from sustainable resources

Contents

director to facilitator • Building vocabularies • Increasing the number of
communication opportunities • Working with large groups • Sustained shared
thinking • Story time • Working in small groups • A whole team approach
• Willingness to reflect • Working with parents

Key of Icons

1 Learning objectives

2 Questions for reflection and discussion

3 Further reading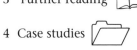

4 Case studies

5 Useful websites

6 Key points for practice

About the Authors

Avril Brock is a Senior Lecturer in the Carnegie Faculty of Sport and Education at Leeds Metropolitan University and is the Award Leader for the MA Childhood Studies and MA Early Years, lecturing on Early Childhood Education. She is in the process of completing her PhD thesis on early years educators' thinking about their professionalism. She published *Into the Enchanted Forest: Drama, Science and Language in Primary Schools* for Trentham Publications in 1999. She has also contributed three chapters to Jean Conteh's (2006) book *Promoting Learning for Bilingual Pupils 3–11: Opening Doors to Success* published by Sage. Avril has been involved in European Union International Projects – Tempus, Socrates, Comenius and Erasmus – for 16 years. She has also formed international partnerships with colleges in California and Boston. Prior to joining Leeds Metropolitan University Avril worked at Bradford College for 15 years lecturing on primary and early years programmes, and before that her teaching career was in schools with linguistically diverse children aged from 3 to 13 years. Her hobbies include travelling and walking and she enjoys being outside in the fresh air as much as possible.

Carolynn Rankin is a Senior Lecturer in the Leslie Silver International Faculty, School of Applied Global Ethics at Leeds Metropolitan University. She is a Chartered Librarian and a Member of the Chartered Institute of Library and Information Professionals (CILIP). Carolynn worked as an information practitioner in a variety of library sectors before joining the School of Information Management at Leeds Metropolitan University in 2000, where she was the Postgraduate Tutor for the CILIP-accredited MSc Information Studies for five years. She has lectured on the management of information and library services and the role of the information professional in developing services to meet community needs. Her current research interests include the role of the early years librarian in multi-disciplinary teamwork and the development of information literacy in communities. She loves giving books as presents and the arrival of a new baby to family or friends is always greeted with delight, as it means a great excuse to spend time in the children's section of her local bookshops.

Contributor

Carol Potter is a Senior Lecturer in Early Childhood Studies at Leeds Metropolitan University, lecturing in the areas of children with disability, autism, language development and engaging fathers in the early years. Carol initially worked as a residential social worker with children with disabilities before training as a nursery teacher, going on to teach young children with autism for several years in the Midlands. Carol then moved into research, first at Northumbria University and then at Durham, where she spent nine years, undertaking a range of projects in the areas of autism as well as language and communication development. Whilst at Durham, Carol worked as a research fellow on a six-year evaluation of a number of local Sure Start programmes in the north of England.

Acknowledgements

This book would not have been written without Jackie Brock, so it is dedicated to her for her perseverance and enthusiasm. Family members, friends, neighbours, colleagues, students, teachers, nursery nurses, managers, early years librarians, parents and staff in many early years settings have contributed to this book.

Particular thanks go to:

Annabelle, William and Claudia; Bev; Branwen; Alana, Carolyn and Richard; Joan; Cynthia, Jamie and Harvey; Darrington Mums and Toddlers Group; David, Kirsty and Melissa; Vicky and George; Dr Sama; Jed and Holly; Jo and Theo; JJ; Maggie Power; Simon, Jackie, Joe and Tom; Stuart, Pauline, Alex and Jack; Susan, Martin, Terrie and Ethan; Denny and Gwen; Emily, her mum and grandma; students at Bradford College and LeedsMet University; Wakefield Libraries and Information Service; Rose Farm Nursery School

What kept the authors going during this journey –

'How do you tell a story? One word at a time ...!

How do you write a book? One word at a time ...!

Now it is written, we hope you enjoy it – one word at a time ...!'

How to Use This Book

With the introduction of the Early Years Foundation Stage in 2008, practitioners need to put the principles into practice and meet the diverse needs of all young children in the six areas of learning – one of which is communication, language and literacy. This book helps readers develop their knowledge, skills and practice in encouraging and promoting communication, language and literacy for babies and young children.

It includes:

- activities, examples, case studies, scenarios and ideas from actual practice
- guidance on how to meet children's diverse needs in an inclusive environment
- advice on involving parents as partners in their children's learning
- information on resources, useful websites and suggestions for further reading.

This book is for practitioners and teachers at all levels – BTEC, NVQ, undergraduate, post-graduate and managers working with young children from birth to age 5. It will help the practitioner to develop partnerships with parents and carers, to provide answers and promote language and literacy experiences, encouraging them to be involved in promoting and understanding their child's language development. This vital link with parents is a recurrent theme and where 'parents' is used throughout the book we mean this to denote 'parents, carers and families'.

The book is full of multilingual ideas and activities as most practitioners work in ethnically diverse settings which constantly have to adapt to support different intakes of children and families. The case studies and scenarios in the book are based on real families interacting with practitioners in a variety of settings, but we have changed all their names.

Each of the seven chapters starts with a boxed summary, and you can see at a quick glance what that chapter will cover. You can also use the contents page to see the sections included in the chapter. Each chapter concludes with 'Questions for reflection and discussion' which can be used for individual review and personal development or as part of a group discussion in a workplace setting or classroom. To encourage your understanding as a practitioner each chapter also has Key Points for practice.

The reference list at the end of the book provides full details of the publications referred to in the chapters so that you can follow up key authors, sources and areas of research. Each chapter also has suggested further reading as a starting point to help you develop your knowledge on the topics, and we have also provided addresses for some useful websites.

Chapter 1 sets the scene on early language development and focuses on why language is so crucial in young children's development and why it is important to build relationships with parents. You will be encouraged to reflect on and evaluate your professional role and its practical application when working with young children.

Chapter 2 demonstrates how intelligent babies are and how they can be very effective communicators from the day they are born, and you will explore first steps into literacy. The importance of parents as partners is featured.

Chapter 3 looks at 'Children's needs: diversity and identity' and will help you to understand how the language and values of home impact upon their learning, to consider gender issues and the special educational needs that affect language development.

Chapter 4 is about the importance of creating high-quality opportunities for communication between adults and young children in early years settings. It will inform you why it is necessary to encourage young children to take the lead in conversations.

Chapters 5 and 6 'Stories, storytelling and books' and 'Rhyme, rhythm, sound and song', provide a wealth of ideas and practical activities supported by the underpinning knowledge about their importance in practice.

Chapter 7 Reading and writing should be fun, and the final chapter, on emerging literacy: playful reading and writing, helps you to make the link to Early Years Foundation Stage.

Appendix 1 provides an introduction to theories of language acquisition. Communication, language and literacy should permeate your provision and Appendix 2 shows a plan for long-term planning in an early years unit.

The index references specific topics and we have provided a glossary to help the reader access the terminology associated with this multi-disciplinary area.

1

Early Language Development

Learning objectives

This chapter focuses on why language is so crucial in young children's development. Effective language use gives babies and children power to have a say in what they want and need. To encourage children's language development, early years practitioners need to optimise their speaking and listening opportunities through everyday conversation and practical activities. Modelling language through meaningful communication is the key. This chapter offers knowledge and understanding of how, why and what to promote for optimum language learning situations and begins to look at the following three vital questions:

- Why is language crucial to young children's development?
- Why is it important to build a relationship with the parents?
- How and why is it useful to analyse young children's language.

Language is crucial to young children's development; it is the essential key for learning, for communicating and building relationships with others as well as for enabling children to make sense of the world around them. Your role in developing and encouraging language acquisition in children is therefore of the utmost importance. However, it is not solely the province of those working with young children, as it is also a concern of parents, carers, families and even policymakers. There is a need for practitioners to disseminate knowledge and good practice to these stakeholders. Those educating young children should be well qualified, but also knowledgeable and well informed about their role. The ability to reflect on and evaluate your professional role and its practical application when working with young children is fundamental. You need to develop and establish an occupational knowledge base that accounts for both professional and practical knowledge. Knowledge and articulation about how young children acquire language and develop into competent thinkers and language users is key to good practice.

Key Elements in Effective Practice

The Key Elements of Effective Practice (KEEP) (DfES 2005) underpin the professional standards for early years practitioners. These competencies are acquired through a combination of skill and knowledge gained through education, training and practical experience. Practitioners need to develop, demonstrate and continuously improve their:

- relationships with both children and adults
- understanding of the individual and diverse ways that children learn and develop
- knowledge and understanding in order to actively support and extend children's learning in and across all areas and aspects of learning and development
- practice in meeting all children's needs, learning styles and interests
- work with parents, carers and the wider community
- work with other professionals within and beyond the setting.

These key elements will permeate this book through concentrating on communication, language and literacy.

An exciting journey

Young children's early years education should be a quality experience for all, be it in a crèche, playgroup, children's centre, nursery or reception class in a school, special educational needs (SEN) setting or with a childminder. The provision of a unified curriculum and equity of experience aims to meet the needs of parents and children in whichever setting they choose. The Early Years Foundation Stage (EYFS) brings together the Birth to Three Matters framework, the Curriculum Guidance for the Foundation Stage (CGFS) and the National Standards for under-8s Day Care and Childminding in a 'single quality framework' for children from birth to the end of the school reception year (DfES, 2007a). Each child and family are seen as unique, with differing needs and concerns. These are identified in the four key themes: A Unique Child; Empowering Relationships; Enabling Environments; Holistic Learning and Developments. The themes are linked to a key principle, each of which has four commitments. Children's development is presented through six phases. These overlap and acknowledge that there can be big differences between the development of children of similar ages (DfES, 2007a). Practitioners plan to enable children to achieve the statutory early learning goals (ELGs) in six areas of learning by the end of the reception year:

- Personal, social and emotional development
- Communication, language and literacy
- Problem solving, reasoning and numeracy
- Knowledge and understanding of the world
- Physical development
- Creative development

Language and communication contributes to all six areas and are key to learning and understanding. The EYFS stresses the importance of providing opportunities for children to communicate thoughts, ideas and feelings, and to build up relationships with practitioners and each other. It also affirms the importance of promoting positive relationships with parents and families. Key workers have an important role in establishing these and ensuring children feel safe, confident and independent. Promoting anti-discriminatory practice is also crucial and practitioners must meet children's needs in terms of ethnicity, culture, religion, home language, family background, special educational needs, disability, gender and ability. We will discuss these issues further in later chapters.

Children learn most effectively through being involved in rich experiences and practical activities promoted through play. Adults need to join in this play, both talking with and listening to the children, taking into account their interests and previous experiences. Children and their families should be involved in these processes. Children need confidence and opportunity to utilise their abilities in a variety of contexts and for a variety of purposes. As a practitioner you can record observations of children's play, learning and language achievements to determine if your provision is high-quality.

How do young children acquire their language? Studying and promoting young children's language development can be an exciting journey. Parents often amuse friends and family by relaying what their children say, yet how do children learn to make these amusing comments, how do they learn to communicate?

There have been several theories about how young children acquire language, but no one perspective on language acquisition tells the whole story. Why not read further about these perspectives in Appendix 1? Each emphasises one aspect or another and there is still a great deal to learn about how it happens and why. We feel the following ideas are the most important for practitioners. Young children acquire language through significant others by interaction in their immediate environment, through responding to sounds, sentences and experiences expressed by their parents, family and other carers. They begin by absorbing, listening and then imitating and practising. Their responses are reinforced by these significant others and patterns begin to emerge, even for the babies, as they try so hard to make sense of what is happening around them. Gradually they learn to reproduce sounds and words and to establish an understanding of how language works, the structure and grammatical sense of putting these sounds and words together. It is generally held that children have an inbuilt language acquisition device (LAD) and/or a language acquisition support system (LASS) that enables this to occur.

Given minimum exposure to language, every child will acquire a sophisticated symbol system to serve its communicative needs. Children gain an understanding about their own particular language and culture, and also knowledge and comprehension of the world around them. Some children will acquire more than one language, sometimes two or three at the same time, sometimes one after another. And among children as a whole, there will be an infinite variety of patterns of language use. Each new experience, whether as children (or adults), extends language skills in some way. Each new creation – a new word, a new way of expressing something – extends the system for the generations that follow. In turn, old ways are replaced with new and so it goes on *ad infinitum*. Such is the power that language offers to children, and such is the power they have over it.

Throughout the book you will glimpse scenarios and case study examples from young children growing up in a variety of linguistic and socio-cultural experiences, in worlds where their first language may not be the national language, in families that are promoting their heritage language, as well as the host country's language, or where signing may be the first or additional language. Languages such as Punjabi, Hindi, Polish, Slovakian, French and Welsh will be mentioned, as well as, of course, English, the main focus of this book. So let us first consider how babies communicate.

Babies' communication

Many parents start communicating with their unborn child in the antenatal stage to cue their baby into their voices and the world around them. Babies cry to attract attention – in this way they communicate with the adults around them to get what they need. They have different cries for different purposes and parents soon get to know which cry means 'I'm hungry', 'I'm in pain', 'I'm damp' or 'Come and play with me now!' Adults respond by meeting these needs and by talking to their baby. So from the very moment they are born children are introduced to the language of their parents. They reciprocate through making eye contact, by gestures, sounds and gurglings, and in so doing soon begin to take part in conversations and thus become communicators.

> Cara was in her car seat at 6 weeks old when I first met her. I chatted to her using sentences such as 'Who's very beautiful then?', 'Aren't you a good girl?', 'Where are you going now?', 'Are you going out in the car with mummy?' As I type these sentences, I think I sound fairly ridiculous – after all what do I expect from a six-week-old baby – full sentences and answers to these questions – a proper conversation? In fact that is just what I did get – well I got 'ooos' and 'aaas'. Cara was already making vowel sounds and she was turn-taking with me – until she got tired, closed her eyes and went to sleep, effectively dismissing me.

When adults hold conversations we take it in turns to speak. Through watching, listening and participating, young children subconsciously learn the conventions of turn-taking. Here Cara is already cueing into this. As she gets older she will intuitively realise that patterns of intonation, pitch, speed and volume also play a part in turn-taking, as do body language and gestures. She will realise that certain phrases also signal whose turn it is to speak.

Adults scaffold their baby's language by interpreting what they might say or need. Throughout these early years, adults will support the baby's attempts at sounds and words, through prompting and repeating. They model appropriate language, providing words and extending the baby's contributions, offering them back in enhanced full sentences. Babies and young children listen avidly – collecting sounds and trialling these themselves.

As they get older babies gain more control over the muscles in their mouths, tongue, throats, lips and pharynx. They begin with vowels sounds, moving to babbling, gurgling and imitating language. The first words are bilabial sounds – 'mmmmm', 'dadadada', 'papapapapa'. It is therefore no surprise that many names for parents are similar in different languages – 'mummy', 'mama', 'maman', 'amma', and 'daddy', 'papa', 'abba'. Babies cue into the sounds of their heritage language or languages of their parents from a very early age. Babies enjoy producing sounds. They will make long continuous repetitions of the same or similar sounds as they babble and gurgle – 'A goi goi goi goi agoi goi goy!' Fortunately babies don't get tired of experimenting and they work extremely hard at their language acquisition.

When communicating and talking to their babies and young children, parents will accommodate their language use to promote attentive listening, understanding and then reproduction of sounds, words, then sentences. Phonetics is the science of speech sounds. Sounds are produced or articulated through the passage of air coming from the lungs via the larynx into the mouth and the movement and positioning of the lips, the tongue, the teeth, and the soft and hard palate. Lips work together to make a wide range of speech sounds. The tongue is very flexible – it adopts many different shapes and positions, including three-dimensional ones. Consonants are made by closing the vocal tract whilst the vowels occur by air escaping unimpeded on the way through the mouth.

Phonology is the study of the sound system, which is the way in which sound is used to express meaning and an analysis of the variations that arise. Sometimes it can be difficult to tell what young children are saying. Even when their vocabulary and syntax are in place, precise pronunciation may take longer and adults have to interpret what is being said and the meanings that are intended. Parents and adults who spend most time with a child will be able to do this more effectively that someone who sees the child intermittently. It is important not to patronise young children. An example of this is:

ADULT: What's your favourite car?
CHILD: A werrarri. [Meaning Ferrari]
ADULT: A werrarri?
CHILD: [*irritated*] No! A werrarri!

Young children's early language development is exciting, interesting and can be amusing. What children say offers a window into their thinking. Figure 1.1 offers are some early pronunciations from Miranda, aged 2 years and 6 months, which demonstrate some of the linguistic processes related to her pronunciation.

Motherese is the adaptation of simplified language by parents in order to communicate with their children. However, parents' language is not absolutely identical in the sense that the father's speech tends to be more direct and uses a wider range of vocabulary than the mother's. It may be more correct to use the term 'parentese', (or infant direct speech) and it can be applicable to any adult carer, relative or friend. Indeed, older children may also do this when talking to younger children. They will perhaps use 'baby talk' or 'talk down' to them by using such vocabulary as 'burny' for hot or 'puddycat' for cat. Animal sounds are also favourites for being simplified; hence the phrases 'gee gee' and 'bow wow'.

Eventually young children will start pointing to things around them and they are actually requesting the adult to supply the name of the object or person. They also will add intonation to help communicate to the adult what they need. As young children begin to 'soak' up the words, it is important to provide them with a rich language environment. As they progress from one word to two words, they add an operator to the name of the object or person, saying 'baby gone', 'look doggy', 'hot daddy'. When young children

What was said	What was meant	Linguistic processes
Ah-dea	Oh dear	Learning pronunciation
Pollypop Wimmin pool	Lollipop Swimming pool	Common mispronunciations
Where Gackie gone? Where Affril gone?	Where have Jackie and Avril gone?	Difficult to pronounce some people's names
'brella	Umbrella	Not pronouncing the beginning of words
Daddy quashing me!	When hugging	'sq' is hard to pronounce
Side and seek; bide and keep; hide and keep	Sometimes hard to tell what she's saying. Adults have to interpret	Pronunciation developing with practice.

Figure 1.1 Examples of Miranda's pronunciation

omit words and talk in short phrases, it is known as telegraphese. Children will also begin to apply the rules of tenses as they gradually acquire them, which is why 'ed' is often added onto irregular verbs. The process of putting the words together to make meaningful sentences is known as syntactic learning, that is, learning to use grammatical rules. Figure 1.2 shows some examples of Miranda's grammar use.

What was said	What was meant	Linguistic processes
Mine broken now Daddy got cup Tent's dark. Lantern on I back this on you	My biscuit is broken now Daddy has got my cup The tent is dark. Put the light on I am putting this hat back on your head	Telegraphese. Knowing the context helps the listener's understanding
My do it	I want to do it	Use of 'my' often comes before use of 'I'
Kirsty tighted me	Fastening into car seat	Generalisation of past tense 'ed'
Me on bus; I wanna bus; Go bus dere; going now. I want blue one. I want to go on bus now	Egocentric, self-maintaining language to get what she wants, to go on the bus	See how the structure and language improves in each phrase
My's porridge	That's my porridge	Applying possession
Make ice cream for you I'm making ice cream for you	I am making ice cream for you	Corrects herself and uses a complete sentence with an auxiliary verb

Figure 1.2 Examples of Miranda's grammar

What was said	What was meant	Linguistic processes
Smack the door/naughty door Baby bit me It's got me	When she bumped into a door When she trod on her doll – it was the doll's fault When her foot got entangled	Personification endowing objects with life Egocentrism: something is else's fault
Small Big Silver	Baby Daddy White	Underextension
Buses and trains All flies Dark colours	Are interchangeable Are spiders Are all black	Overgeneralisations
Not shirt. It top	Corrected Daddy when he talked about his top as a shirt, because shirts have to have buttons	Becoming very specific in her concepts
Dark in there	When she has sunglasses on	Literal understanding, making sense
Blue tea	Orange juice with a slice of lemon	Miranda's conceptualisation: creating meaning and making sense

Figure 1.3 Examples of Miranda's meaning making

Young children are not only acquiring vocabulary, they are also learning about concepts and trying to make sense of the world. It often sounds as though they are getting things wrong, but listen carefully to see how children are interpreting what is going on around them. Underextension is the limiting of the meaning of the word to the child's own narrow worldview. For example 'car' may refer only to the 'family car' or slippers may refer only to 'daddy's slippers'. Overextension on the other hand is when a child is applying a wider meaning to the word than is usual in adult language, such as 'car' referring to all road vehicles or 'cat' to all animals. This process of understanding concepts and putting vocabulary together to make sense and meaning is known as semantic learning. Some examples from Miranda are given in Figure 1.3.

Miranda's father had been concerned that she was slow to start speaking. However, at the age of 2 years and 8 months this little girl had become quite a conversationalist. She could sit at the dinner table all evening with six adults, holding conversations, alternating between talking to herself in monologues and demanding that the adults participate in role-play games. Her father feels that being surrounded and immersed in language makes a huge difference. At first it was hard for adults other than her father to understand her, but during the course of the next few months her pronunciation would become clearer, and her vocabulary and syntax would grow. She quickly developed into a competent language user.

There is a lot involved in this acquisition of language. Young children have to produce the sounds, learn the words and their meanings and put them together in a correct sentence structure. They also have to acquire the factors involved in social interaction; the social rules that affect the choices of language – the vocabulary; grammatical constructions; pronunciation; accent and dialect. This is known as the pragmatics of language use.

First attempts at language for all children go through similar phases of development. Gordon Wells constructed five stages of language development (see Figure 1.4), paying

Function What children are trying to do with their language	Meaning The states, events, relationships the children talk about	Structure The way in which language is put together: grammar	STAGE
Gain attention Direct attention to object or event Get something they want Make basic statements Make requests	Naming things Connecting objects and people: Mummy's car; There Nana; Ball gone. Much meaning conveyed by intonation	Single words – look; more; there; want. These are called operators and convey whole of the meaning Name and operator: Look bird; Doggy gone; There Daddy	I
Asking questions – mainly 'Where?'	Naming and classifying: constantly asking 'Wassat?' Changing locations: people coming, going, getting up or down. Attributes: hot; cold; big; small; naughty doggy; It cold Mummy	Interrogative pronoun: Where book? 'A' and 'the' commence in front of nouns. Basic sentences of noun and verb: Car gone; Baby drink. Possession through the apostrophe begins: Jack's chair; Teddy's sweeties	II
Explosion of questions, often through intonation 'Play, Mummy?'	Talk about actions which change object acted upon: 'You dry hands'. Use verbs like 'listen' and 'know' referring to events in past and sometimes in the future. Ongoing actions: 'Me doing it'; 'Mark still in bed'. Enquire state of actions such as if something is finished. Talk about things changing.	Sentence structure now: subject + verb + object + addition: 'You dry hands': 'A man dig down there'. Use of auxiliary verbs: 'I am going'. Preposition + article + noun: 'in the cupboard'.	III
Complex sentence-use Make a range of requests: Shall I do it? Can I have that? Make and ask for explanations. The 'why?' question appears	Now convey a wide range of complex meanings. Use of abstract psychological verbs such as 'know'; expressing thinking and understanding. Express meaning indirectly: 'Can I have?' replaces 'Give me' Expressing meaning appropriately in context.	'Can I have one?' 'He doesn't want one?' No longer need intonation to convey meaning. Now able to use auxiliary verbs: do; can; will. References through sentence: 'I want the pen Grandad gave me'; 'I know you're there'.	IV

Function What children are trying to do with their language	Meaning The states, events, relationships the children talk about	Structure The way in which language is put together: grammar	STAGE

Can now:
– give information
– ask and answer varied
  questions
– request directly and
  indirectly
– suggest
– offer
– state and ask about own
  and other people's
  intentions, express
  feelings and attitudes
	Hypothetical and
	conditional statements: 'If
	you do that, I will . . .'
	Refer to past and future
	times specifically: 'after tea'.
	Formulate conditions for
	something to happen:
	'You've got to switch that
	on first'.
	Talk about state of affairs.
	Make estimations.
		Questions of 'what?', 'when?'
		and 'what does it mean?'
		Invert subject and verb in
		'When is she coming?'
		Can create complex
		sentences of several clauses.
		Now greater flexibility in
		sentences; not just adding
		to length of sentence but
		can now structure meaning
		economically. More
		cohesive in language use.
			V

Figure 1.4 Five stages of language development

Source: Adapted from Wells (1985) and Language in the National Curriculum (unpublished, 1990)

attention to the function, meaning and structure of young children's early language acquisition. However he determined that it was important not to attach an age range to these stages. Children will progress through all these stages, but may have different rates of achievement according to their own personal development.

Children will undoubtedly understand more than they can express and demonstrate the meaning of in everyday language use. By the end of Stage V (5) a child's language is firmly in place with a vocabulary of several thousand words. It is evident that the opportunity to hear and use language for a wide range of purposes, audiences and contexts directly affects the rate and expertise of children's future language development.

The rest of this chapter focuses attention on key features of the process of language development by using the example of one particular child, Miranda. This is to demonstrate language development in action and promote both practical and professional knowledge and understanding. It provides a method for *what to promote*, *what to observe* and *how to record*.

 A year's development at nursery – Miranda, age 2 years 6 months

This case study aims to demonstrate three things:

- One young child's language in the first three of her early years
- How to relate her language and experiences to the EYFS
- How to analyse these experiences and target future opportunities for development

Miranda started Robin House nursery in November 2004 when she was 10 months 3 weeks old. The nursery's first profile of Miranda, compiled through contributions from her mother, is shown in Figure 1.5.

> **Miranda Lawrence**
>
> Prior to starting nursery, Miranda came for visits with mum, which went well. She can sometimes get a little upset when parted from her parents but can easily be distracted and settled. Miranda is now feeling confident enough to go off by herself and explore the room, but likes to have an adult close by for reassurance and cuddles.
>
> Miranda enjoys messy activities. She joined in with the floor painting session and she will play in the sand for long periods. Miranda is a lovely little girl who likes lots of cuddles.
>
> **I would like to tell you about my routine:**
> I tend to have a nap after lunchtime although I am difficult to get to sleep. I play with my toys best during the morning. In the afternoon I like more company. I like to look at books and have cuddles during this time and also play with my dolly.
>
> **Things that comfort me:**
> Music. Someone singing 'Somewhere over the rainbow' or the 'Bare Necessities' from The Jungle Book.
> Looking out of windows and having things pointed out.
> Looking at microwaves distracts me.

Figure 1.5: Miranda's first profile at nursery

Miranda's key worker undertook regular recorded observations of her achievements. A selection of these are outlined in Figures 1.7 and 1.8.

- First year at nursery: themes and commitments
- Second year at nursery: working towards communication, language and literacy goals

Although her development was originally analysed according to the Birth to Three Matters curriculum, it is presented here with regard to the EYFS. This is done to demonstrate how you can undertake analysis with reference to the new curriculum. There are four themes within the Early Years Foundation Stage and how each of these incorporates the four commitments is shown in Figure 1.6.

The examples given in this case study have been selected from a wealth of the nursery's observations. The focus is on communication and language development and it will be seen that there are strong connections across each of the four themes in relation to language. In order for observations to be useful, they need not only to be a record of achievement, but also to be analysed to ensure there is a holistic record of a child's development. It is also important to look for areas that need to be encouraged. Observations should be undertaken to record what a child is achieving in everyday activities and when something interesting happens.

The following observations track Miranda during her first years at nursery from the age of 11 months to 2 years 6 months. In Figure 1.7 her development can be seen through showing:

Themes	Commitments			
A Unique Child	Child Development	Inclusive Practice	Keeping Safe	Health and Well-Being
Positive Relationships	Respecting Each Other	Parents as Partners	Supporting Learning	Key Person
Enabling Environments	Observation, Assessment and Planning	Supporting Every Child	The Learning Environment	The Wider Context
Learning and Development	Play and Exploration	Active Learning	Creativity and Critical Thinking	Areas of Learning and Development

Figure 1.6: The four themes within the Early Years Foundation Stage
Source: DfES (2007a)

- Aspects from the Early Years Foundation Stage
- Observation of the actual event, experience or activity
- Analysis of what is happening

The observations, analysis and targets demonstrate the importance of noting children's accomplishments and development to ensure they gain a depth and breadth of learning experiences. Whilst these are focused on the themes and commitments in the EYFS, the interrelationship with communication, language and literacy is evident within them all. The majority of observations demonstrate aspects of Miranda's interaction with others as she forms more social and confident relationships. In her second year she uses more verbal language to communicate with her peers and adults. Pay particular attention to these aspects as you look at Miranda's second year at nursery (Figure 1.8) and see if you can determine how they relate to communication, language and literacy.

Photo record with empathy doll: role-playing mum

Miranda's first year at nursery		
Theme	Observation	Analysis
A Unique Child Child Development	Miranda spots a cat on the windowsill, points to it and exclaims, 'Cat'.	Using one word level language to convey simple meanings.
A Unique Child Inclusive Practice	Miranda is sitting on the settee looking at books.	Early reading, handling and enjoying books.
A Unique Child Keeping Safe	Miranda is playing with a doll's house when another child comes to take her doll. Miranda says, 'Mine'.	Demonstrating self-awareness, able to communicate feelings. Learning about boundaries and when to say 'No'.
A Unique Child Health and Well-Being	Miranda cuddles another child, who is upset.	Awareness of the needs of others. Shows empathy to others
Positive Relationships Respecting Each Other	Miranda is playing with a musical toy, which she takes to play with another child.	Confident with her peers. Acknowledging others.
Positive Relationships Parents as Partners	Miranda chats and plays with an adult as they sing 'Row, row, row your boat'.	Playing with an adult, talking and communicating.
Positive Relationships Supporting Learning	Miranda smiles and laughs with delight while singing. The other children applaud her.	Confident as part of the group and when singing the core songs.
Positive Relationships Key Person	Miranda looks at 'Five Little Ducks' book with an adult. She points to a picture saying 'Duck' and 'Quack'.	Using words in context, associating pictures, meaning and onomatopoeia.
Enabling Environments Observation, Assessment and Planning	Miranda plays with cornflour; watching, catching and exploring its texture and smell.	Responding with her senses.
Enabling Environments Supporting Every Child	Miranda joins in pretend play at the hospital.	Using gestures and actions. Developing relationships.
Enabling Environments The Learning Environment	Miranda climbs into the sand and uses her whole body to explore it.	Exploring the environment confidently.
Enabling Environments The Wider Context	Miranda takes care of the empathy doll, changing its pants on a mat.	Re-enacting familiar scenes, practising role-play situations and role-playing mum.

Theme	Observation	Analysis
Learning and Development Play and Exploration	Miranda takes clothes out of the washing machine. Puts a pan of play-dough in saying, 'Its hot, hot!'	Demonstrating awareness of potential danger. Being imaginative with materials and enacting familiar activities.
Learning and Development Active Learning	Miranda walks over the bridge unaided, climbs onto the step, then back down the steps backwards.	Exploring the outdoors with confidence, exercising excellent gross motor skills.
Learning and Development Creativity and Critical Thinking	Miranda squirts paint onto paper. Puts her hands in and makes hand print designs.	Confident using materials. Expresses creativity and shows initiative in her actions.
Learning and Development Areas of Learning and Development	Miranda soothes a crying child, stroking his hair and back, then putting her finger to her lips and saying, 'Shhh!'	Comforting another child, demonstrating care and affection. Acting responsibly.

Figure 1.7: How to analyse a child's communication and language: Model A

Figure 1.8 shows:
- Communication, language and literacy objectives
- Observation of what is happening
- Analysis of what it shows
- Future aspects for development

Miranda's second year at nursery

Communication, language and literacy: Objectives	Observation: What is happening?	What this shows	What could be done next?
Make up songs, rhymes and poems	Miranda asked to play with the drums during music time.	Communicating with adults. Experiencing music and rhythm.	Opportunities to express personal preferences.
Show an understanding of the elements of stories Know that print carries meaning	Miranda and Jaydee share the crib in the home corner and read together.	Showing self-assurance. Sharing and enjoying books and stories.	Develop book-handling skills.
Enjoy listening to and using spoken language in play	Miranda pedals around a child shouting 'passing you'.	Learning to consider others.	Encourage communication about actions.

Communication, language and literacy: Objectives	Observation: What is happening?	What this shows	What could be done next?
Listen with enjoyment, and respond to stories, songs and other music, rhymes and poems	Miranda joins in as Lee plays music and sings along to the CD.	Expressing herself through song, gesture and movement.	Provide lots of music experiences.
Speak clearly and audibly with confidence and control and show awareness of the listener	As a parent left Miranda waved and said, 'Goodbye'.	Exhibiting the impulse to communicate with others.	Promote opportunities for interaction.
Sustain attentive listening, responding to what they have heard with relevant comments, questions or actions	Miranda completed a jigsaw, clapping at her achievement. She repeated the adult's, 'Well done, Miranda!'	Listening and responding to what others say, making meaningful responses.	Provide time for building communicative relationships.
Enjoy listening to and using spoken word and readily turn to it in their play	Miranda and Lee in the home corner pretending to drink from tins. 'Mine tea'.	Communicating and negotiating with others.	Promote time and opportunities for conversations.
Use talk to organise, sequence and clarify thinking, ideas, feelings and events	Miranda saw someone wearing pink doodle shoes and correctly said 'Same as Emily's'.	Being able to compare and classify objects.	Promote more times for finding out about others.
Interact with others, negotiating plans and activities and taking turns in conversation Explore and experiment with sounds	Miranda moved the chairs into a row and enlisted the help of friends to go on 'choo choo train' with her.	Role-playing in groups. Moving objects to produce desired effect.	Offer materials for role-playing trains. Support onomatopoeia.
Extend their vocabulary, exploring the meanings and sounds of new words	Miranda made pancakes out of play-dough, tossing them in frying pan. 'Pancake fly'.	Making discoveries, developing competence, being resourceful.	Provide further opportunities for using imaginative language.
Attempt writing for different purposes	Miranda uses two brushes to make lines and patterns using the whole of the paper, concentrating hard and being careful.	Exploring and experimenting with colour and patterns, creating own marks and lines.	Provide signs and symbols to imitate.

Communication, language and literacy: Objectives	Observation: What is happening?	What this shows	What could be done next?
Use language to imagine and recreate roles and experiences	At teatime, Miranda feeds the empathy doll a cracker. 'Teatime baby. Eat up.'	Developing caring skills. Links language to actions and role-play.	Promote new vocabulary.
Use a pencil and hold it effectively	Threads pasta to make a rakhi wristband, paints with a brush, draws pictures of family and builds a robot.	Developing motor skills, fine manipulation and hand–eye co-ordination.	Promote lots of manipulation experiences.
Speak clearly and audibly with confidence and control and show awareness of the listener	Miranda plays peek-a-boo with Nicko in sensory room giggling 'Your turn now!'	Seeking and experiencing closeness with others.	Allow opportunities for conversing and interacting.
Attempt writing for different purposes	Miranda joins Harry making, patterns in fork with play-dough: 'My's pattern good'.	Collaborative mark making.	Provide more mark-making experiences.

Figure 1.8 How to analyse a child's communication and language: Model B

These observations have been condensed for ease of presentation as many more detailed accounts were recorded throughout Miranda's second year at nursery. This sample gives an idea of how to document achievements. The emphasis has been on her communication – on oral language development. Several of the literacy goals will need to be targeted in more detail in her subsequent years in the foundation stage. Miranda still has a long time before she has to achieve all the early learning goals at the end of her Reception year. The tables illustrated in this case study offer you varied ways of recording accomplishments. You need to determine the most effective ways of observing, recording and analysing children's development and achievements, being aware of what to promote to create optimum language-learning experiences.

At Miranda's nursery all observations, profiles, photographs, pictures and assessments are given to parents so that they have a full record of their child's life at nursery. This should be a two-way process and parents should have a role in contributing to these. Miranda's father is definitely very proud of his daughter and treasures these records.

The learning journey

So far we have demonstrated the observations and analysis of Miranda's language learning through short scenarios. There are other ways of recording young children's language learning through documenting their learning journey. North Yorkshire's Early Years Services promote four stages of documenting children's learning:

- describing how children learn
- discussing what has been learnt
- documenting the activities and learning
- deciding what to do next.

The emphasis is on dialogic talk about learning. They advocate looking at children's dispositions and motivation through recording the narrative, that is, telling a story of the context, relationships, concentration and persistence, using photographs and video to capture verbal and non-verbal communications. The focus is on the learning more than on the child's achievements, on what they are interested in, and it involves both the children themselves and their families and in this way, you will be able to plan for activities for children that will deepen their interest. It is also important to allow children to reflect on their own learning. Documenting learning with photographs will offer children the wherewithal for them to think and talk about what they are doing by engaging them in the narratives and dialogues. There are many further case studies and scenarios offered throughout the next chapters that will provide you with examples of how to celebrate each child's learning. They will also enable you to reflect on your own practice.

All children will be learning their first or additional language in the same way and will go through the same processes and phases irrespective of the targeted language. What is important to remember however, is though all children follow similar patterns of development, the age and rate at which they develop may differ. This can be influenced by different factors:

- Home environment and the time spent with carers who talk to children
- The number of language-rich experiences
- The learning of two languages simultaneously
- State of children's emotional well-being
- Intellectual development resulting from both environmental and genetic factors
- Physical health and whether children have any hearing, visual or speech impairments
- Premature birth, which may account for some language delay

 Questions for reflection and discussion

- Think about your ability to reflect on and evaluate your professional role and its practical application when working with young children.
- How can you promote positive relationships with parents and families and inform them about their child's achievements?
- Think about recording observations of children's play focusing on their language achievements.
- Determine the most effective ways of observing, recording and analysing children and how to promote optimum language learning experiences.

Key points for practice

- Provide optimum experiences for young children's language development.
- Offer a language-rich environment.
- Model language through meaningful communication.
- Know how to support and promote effective development.
- Support and advise parents.
- Be aware of young children's family and cultural experiences.

 Further Reading

Buckley, B. (2003) *The Children's Communication Skills – From Birth to Five Years.* London: Routledge Falmer.
Riley, J. (2006) *Language and Literacy* 3–7. London: PCP.
Sage, R. (2006) *Supporting Language and Communication: A Guide for School Support Staff.* London: PCP.

 Useful websites

www.teachernet.gov.uk/teachingandlearning/EYFS/profile
www.surestart.gov.uk/improvingquality/ensuringquality/eyfs
www.earlylearningforums.co.uk
www.tactyc.org.uk
www.early-education.org.uk

2

Babies Are Clever

 Learning objectives

The Effective Provision of Pre-School Education (EPPE 1997–2004) research demonstrated the importance of parents in children's early educational achievements. This chapter demonstrates how intelligent babies are and how they can be effective communicators from the day they are born. Language does not take place solely through talk, and this chapter shows the different ways babies can communicate. First steps into literacy are explored showing how babies enjoy books and how and why they are being invited into libraries! Partnership is a two-way process as practitioners and parents can learn from each other. This chapter contains good advice which should ensure you are all involved in children's language development. It looks at:

- How babies communicate.
- How babies' language development can be stimulated and encouraged.
- How you can promote active partnerships with parents.

Babies are thinkers

It is now known that babies can hear before they are born, but did you know that they can actually begin to discern their own mother's voice from as early as 16 weeks from conception? While the foetus is in the womb the sound waves from the mother's voice pass through her body, which means that the baby is repeatedly hearing the same voice. This has important implications for the baby's language acquisition. By week 27, even the baby's cry is already beginning to incorporate some of the voice patterns, rhythms and features of their mother's speech. It means that babies can naturally begin to acquire their heritage language well before they make their entrance onto the world's stage. This also explains why babies born to English speaking parents prefer to hear the English language and will look at people who are speaking that language. In the same way, Japanese babies will look at people who are speaking the Japanese language. The sounds are familiar to them and they naturally gravitate towards what is recognisable and therefore feels safe and comfortable.

Parents often ask whether it is a good idea to talk to their unborn baby. It is known that babies can discern their mother's voice even before their entry into the world. The sound waves pass through the mother's body to the baby, who is gradually able to filter out the background noise and pick up the mother's voice.

Brain development in the early years

Neurophysiology is the study of the body's nervous system. We learn as we interact with the world and the stimulation of neurons in the body and brain passes messages along from one to another. This networking of the neurons effectively produces thought – the source of language. From thought comes meaning and it is meaning that helps us to understand and interpret the world – the ultimate goal of any learning experience. Each new experience adds to previous ones to create a rich tapestry of learning and communication.

Research in the field of developmental psychology shows that the interactions that occur between young children and their carers are important. They not only promote close relationships and early language development but also contribute to children's intellectual development. There are now many studies on the development of the brain that suggest that a young child's early years is an important time for brain development and functioning. Neurological research has confirmed the importance of learning in the early years (Sylva and Pugh, 2005). You can reassure parents that it is never too late to start talking to their baby. The baby may not be able to speak but it will certainly respond to the sound of your voice with smiles, hand movements and facial expressions.

Recently, research has been conducted to show that brain gym can enhance the brain's performance. Brain gym can involve providing a multi-sensory environment incorporating touch, sight, smell and listening. This is something from which babies can also benefit. It is important for babies to have the following natural experiences and types of brain gym that will encourage thinking, learning and communication:

- Have interaction with adults as listeners
- Practise the same movements, sounds and rhythms
- Practise language patterns repeatedly
- Have opportunities for imaginative play
- Discover and investigate creative means of expressing themselves
- Be able to move around on their tummies to explore their personal space and the physical environment around them

Schemas

Schemas are repeated actions or behaviour from experiences that gradually develop into co-ordinated and assimilated activities (Athey, 2007). Piaget initially observed these types of actions in young children and recognised them as being part of the development of the cognitive function of children's minds. However, more recent research has identified these actions in babies and toddlers as an integral element of their learning process. Observers can readily pinpoint 'schemas' in babies' actions as they see them suck, pull, handle or tug on objects, or gaze unmoving on people or things for prolonged periods of time, or in toddlers as they repeatedly move items around and play in certain ways. Such activities gradually take on greater cohesion and connectedness enabling babies and young toddlers to become more co-ordinated and more easily able to manipulate their own movements (see Nutbrown, 2006).

Babies are imitators

The following case study shows how babies operate in their home environment.

 ### Elena, age 14 months

Elena, has just moved into her new home and is very protective of 'her' house. She did not like the decorator and by the second day is shouting 'ra ra ra ra ra ra ra' at him. It is baby talk but the tone of her voice, the finger wagging and how she waves her hands round before stomping off, make it clear what she wants to communicate. As a baby, Elena always made lots of sounds – gurgling and babbling and, once she discovered her voice, became very vocal. She makes lots of sounds in her own conversation as she plays and says things such as 'go u de pu da da un' and tries to make lots of different sounds into sentences – 'hum ha ha ha hum'. She thinks she is saying exactly what she wants to say. Elena is inquisitive and wants to know the names of things. She points to objects for the adult to say the word – says 'What's that' which actually sounds like 'that'. Mum supplies the answer to the pointing as Elena wants to know exactly what it is: three cats, five bears, nine bees – in the pictures in the bedroom – or at breakfast time: bowl, table, cup, milk. Elena copies everything she sees – brushing her hair, cleaning the floor, putting the phone to mummy's ear. She is the 'baby' in the mirror and she kisses her own reflection She loves talking to daddy on the phone, it is baby talk but she natters away for a long time – 'ra ra ra ra ra' – blows kisses and laughs. Elena can follow instructions and understands a lot. Her mum emphasises words for her at every opportunity, repeating words and phrases – 'What is it? Who is it? Is it doggy?' Mum offers continual praise through 'good girl', 'clever girl' and 'Ah beautiful'. Elena is also very capable in using paralinguistics and intonation and often communicates through looks, shrugs, coughs, smiles, sighs, huffs and puffs. Even at 14 months she knows and recognises her friends Shaun and Cameron and they greet each other with hugs, then try to push each other over! Pragmatics are the factors involved in social interaction; social rules that affect our choices of language, the vocabulary, grammatical constructions, accent and dialect and pronunciation. Elena is becoming adept at all these aspects of language.

It is fascinating to discover and record a baby's first words (see Elena's in Figure 2.1) and to make comparisons with other babies – not for competition to see who is saying the most and at what age, but more to determine what each child's first experiences are and which words they will favour first. For example if there are no animals in the family home or vicinity, then it is unlikely 'cat' and 'dog' will be first words. Figure 2.2 shows Agata's first words at 13 months – she lives in Poznan in Poland.

Word	Meaning
Dadadadadadadadadadadda	Daddy
[Doesn't say mum]	[Mum is always there]
Book	Book
Ba	Ball
At	Cat
That	What's that?
Gaden	Garden
Yeah	Yes
No; not	No
Gangi	Grandad
Da	Door
Pi – ur –	Picture [ct – very hard]

Figure 2.1 Elena's first words

Word	Meaning
Ta Ta	Daddy
Mama	Mummy
Da da	Bye bye
How-how	Dog
Miau miau	Cat
Chota? Cioto?	Co to jest? [What is it?]
Bam	Fall down
Czesc	Hi [understands but doesn't say it yet]
KU-KU	I see [peekaboo]
Jaja	Dziadzia [Grandad]
Be Be	Not good for you; something is wrong; warning
Baba	Grandmother

Figure 2.2 Agata's first words

This act of communication is the same in whichever language and whichever country or culture children grow and develop. Babies and young children need people to communicate with, to talk to and to do things to talk about. Language and communication occurs in the home, in an early years setting, in the playground, at a restaurant. Babies need language-rich experiences and activities.

Monique at 17 months wandered around the restaurant in Thailand with her parents taking it in turn to follow closely behind. She is very social and communicates both with the people sitting at the tables and the starlings flying in and out of the veranda. She calls 'aaaahhh, aaaahhh, aaahhh, aaaahhh' to the birds, putting a whole range of intonation patterns and expressions into her calls. Monique shakes hands with and waves goodbye to the humans. Whilst she is expressing herself in single words and sounds, her parents talk in full sentences all the time, modelling language through appropriate vocabulary and grammatical structures. 'Quelle dommage! L'oiseau est ici – regarde l'oiseau.'

It was such an interesting episode, not only because of Monique's developing language, but also that many diners were watching her; that she was charming and that she was so obviously delighting in talking to the birds and exploring her immediate environment.

Babies and dads

Fathers have a role to play and can do anything that a mother can do, aside from breast feeding! It is important that dad is involved in bathing, feeding, dressing, telling stories and chatting to the baby. The more that dad interacts with the baby now, the easier it will be to develop a relationship with the child later in life. A father who is looking forward to taking his son to watch football on Saturday as a teenager needs to start working on the relationship today.

Mark spends as much time as he can with his son, Ewan. As he works evenings and nights, it means that he has time through the day when Ewan is alert and awake. At 5 months old, Ewan really enjoys imitating and copying everything around him. He is also inquisitive and wants to touch and examine anything within reach. Whilst lying on the rug he stretches for his rattle and his requests get louder and louder. There is quite a lot of turn-taking and it's hard to know who is imitating whom – Ewan leading and Mark following or *vice versa*. There are lots of vowel sounds, gurgling, sighing and heavy breathing coming from Ewan (see Figure 2.3). Mark throws Ewan around and engages in rough and tumble play, all the time talking to him, making close eye contact and drawing him close, up and down. This physical play and turn-taking in this way is something that fathers are often very good at.

Ewan	Mark
Come to daddy	Aaaaaaaaaaaaaa
Come on to daddy	Hahhhaaah eeee
Yeah, good boy	Goigoigoi
What?	Aaaaaaaaaa
Come on little boy	Ooooooooooo.
What's the matter?	Hahaha [sighs]
Where's he gone? Boo!	Whooooooo.
He's gone. Wooooooshssh	Oooooooo
Do you want to stand up?	Oooooooo
What are you doing?	Goigoigoi
What are you doing?	Aaaaaaaaaa
Are you trying to do that?	Oooooooo
Are you trying to do it?	Oooooerrrrrrr

Figure 2.3 Father and baby son turn-taking in conversation

Babies are communicators

Conversation is actually a complex act of communication. Speech can be informal, spontaneous, rapid, loosely connected, and involve non-standard forms. Subject matter can be erratic – the topics are not normally planned. There may be repetition, false starts, pauses and hesitations in performance; mmmmmms, ummms, ers. Participants both listen and talk, paying attention to what the other participant is saying. Memory, attention and perception are all involved. There may be code switching between formal/informal language, accent/dialect and even between two languages. This deixis is rooted in time and place of the conversation, in shared knowledge about each other, about the present context and in previous and shared cultural experiences. As children develop language use, they begin to use processes that make for a greater economy of expression, collectively referred to as cohesion. Parents often ask questions about the use of dummies (comforters). They can be barriers to clear talking and it can be a source of frustration to the listener who cannot understand the words that are not properly pronounced. Using a dummy can also affect teeth shape and muscle development.

Babies enjoy massage

There are many benefits to baby massage. It is good for the parent and child to bond as they spend this quality time together. It encourages communication between the parent and baby through talking, eye contact or physical contact – both visual and tactile communication. It promotes eye contact and communication, often through sounds, particularly vowels, and copying. It can improve babies' behaviour and create a stronger relationship, so that within six weeks there can be a vast difference: babies immediately relax when they enter the massage room, request to have their nappy off and look for their 'friends'. Baby massage is fun for both the parent and child, important for relaxation together and can even help to combat postnatal depression. It stimulates the baby's muscles and senses, which is particularly important for babies with special needs, such as Down's syndrome. Baby massage can improve circulation, breathing, digestion and even growth in the baby. Vicky relates the benefit she discovered through attending baby massage classes with her daughter. Eight-month-old Alicia enjoyed baby massage for the four-week course and on completion it became part of their daily routine before bedtime:

> When I ask Alicia 'Can I massage your leg?' she responds immediately by lifting one leg. While I am still in the process of giving an Indian massage to that leg, she will begin to poke me with the other leg as if to communicate, 'Come on mum, what about his one?' It is her way of communicating with me, trying to get my attention. Throughout the massage her eyes are transfixed on me and she chatters away, clearly enjoying the experience. I noticed the change in the other babies too during the course. Many mums and babies would arrive feeling tense and nervous, but within a few weeks the babies began to strip off their clothes, relax and enjoy the experience. The bonding and communication had fantastic effects on the relationships.

Babies signing

Signing is another method that can encourage babies to communicate. Talking requires the co-ordination of many facial muscles and it can take babies up to a year to be able to say their first word and up to two years to be able to string together a full sentence. Signing is a way of teaching babies to communicate before they can talk. It can help reduce the frustration experienced by a baby who cannot yet communicate her wants or needs. Babies can learn to sign from as early as eight months old. Although the length of time it takes for a child to learn how to sign back will vary, most children will learn to reciprocate within 6 to 12 weeks. When a baby learns to sign that she needs a drink, it eradicates the necessity to shout, scream and snatch, meaning that not only is the child less stressed but so are her parents. It could be argued that a potential disadvantage of signing is that it will make the child lazy and eliminate the need to learn how to talk. However, the evidence is to the contrary. Parents who have used this approach as a method of communication maintain that their child became more eager to learn to talk and the speed of language acquisition was accelerated.

Twins

Twins are so interesting – do they know they are twins, do they communicate with each other and will they develop their own language? Here is Andrea talking about her 5-month-old twins, Carl and Clara:

> Yes, to all three questions. They definitely communicate with each other and they do know they are twins. On a morning when they wake they mutter to each other in their own language and they'll lay quite happy together. They look and smile at each other and when they're on the playmat they touch. When they see other babies they look bemused, but they definitely know each other. They are contented together much more than other babies, they look at other babies and are happy to be with them, happy to socialise. I think they're already ahead socially because they are used to being with each other. They're very good – when I fed them this morning, I was feeding Carl and singing to him and Clara was watching happily and then when I changed them over he is equally happy. They definitely seem happier together, than when you're on your own with one. They love you singing and dancing with them. They laugh all the time. They love '3, 2, 1, launch' and then we throw them into the air and they know, they laugh and anticipate and they get excited. Carl particularly understands, he listens to you and gets excited when you get to '1'. He makes the most noises – he goes 'agoo'; and when he sneezes he goes 'aaaaa'. When they're in bed we both burst out laughing because we can hear them taking turns making sound – 'rrrraaarrrraaa orrooraaaaa aaaayyyyaaaa'. They make the funniest noises to each other.

Environments for babies

It is important to give babies opportunities to interact with others on a regular basis. There are now many opportunities for parents and babies to socialise and communicate with other families. The following are settings or groups that have activities for babies:

Where do babies socialise?

- Children's centre
- Playgroup
- Crèche
- Mother and baby/toddler groups
- Nursery
- Community centre
- Library
- Baby cinema
- Play centre
- Toy library
- Coffee mornings
- Sports centre and swimming pool
- Health centre

What activities can they do?

- Music and movement, baby gym, Joe Jingles, Moving Minnies
- Baby massage
- Swimming and baby aqua
- Singing time
- Signing class
- Yoga for babies
- Baby cinema
- Breast feeding group
- Rhyme and story time

The mums and toddlers group in one village is a lively vibrant place to be on a Thursday morning. It is a commuter village and people move around in their cars, so it was a surprise to discover so many families with young children living in the village. One grandma commented 'Aren't I sad, I've still come even though the grandchildren are away on holiday!' Tea and coffee are provided on arrival and there is lots of chat between adults and children. The 3-year-olds get involved in play activities, the toddlers move around in walkers or by crawling and the youngest babies watch everything from floor level on a rug near mums and dads. After free play, there is snack time and they socialise round the table, followed by painting and then song and rhyme time. The organisers are volunteers and as they and their children move on, they target the next suitable coordinator. Here is one mother's experience:

> We moved into the village three years ago and after bumping into an old school friend I was invited to attend mums and tots. After I had Gary, the other mums asked me to take on the organisation of the group. I have to attend every week and it is hard work organising, thinking of input and contributing each week. I am often exhausted by the end of the session, but it is totally rewarding. I really feel that I am making a difference in the community, encouraging people to make friends and to get to know each other, plus the children absolutely love it. There is always an excellent turn out. The whole community is involved, including mums, dads and grandmas. Children feel more part of it because the family is involved in the community and volunteering.

Babies love stories, songs and rhymes

> It is amazing how gratified you can feel to engage a baby in a storytelling experience that he or she is wholeheartedly enjoying. Why is it that a baby's smile feels like a reward?
>
> Josh was only four months old and was already having a wealth of story experiences. We were having a pub lunch when I told him my own version of the story 'How much do I love you?' It is such an expressive story. Both the repetitive language, and the way the story promotes a rise and fall of pitch and voice, held his attention. Josh gazed at me intently, with large eyes listening to the intonation of these phrases. I held his attention for quite a long time.

At one setting, practitioners use magnetic story boards. Stories, songs and rhymes are brought alive through visual and auditory means as the children hold the magnetic characters, communicating, sharing and collaborating with each other. The babies get excited at magnetic song time and will go and collect a particular song bag to initiate the song. One little girl was so excited in anticipation of the song she was bouncing up and down and shaking her arms. The babies recognise the tunes and the objects. Very young children join in with their eyes, scream, clap and shout 'all gone'. There is total interaction and a lot of happy children. What a multisensory experience! This example will be further explored in Chapter 6.

Babies and books

Reading to babies and getting them involved with books is one of the most effective ways of enhancing language development. Babies can learn to handle books and acquire vocabulary as parents and carers provide the words that match the pictures, they can learn animal sounds and start to make the growling, hissing, squeaking and baaing noises using a range of sounds and beginning voice gymnastics with enthusiasm.

Amy illustrates the importance of involving babies in choosing books to read. Although the baby may not yet be able to understand the words or articulate formulated responses, clearly she is enjoying the experience. She is looking at the pictures and learning how to turn the pages. At times, looking at the book together may stimulate a response – a gurgling, or cooing sounds or an attempt to point at pictures on the page. Amy's mother tells us something about how they share the reading experience:

> Reading a book together now forms part of our daily routine. There is a large box full of books and before bed every night we choose a book to read together. Sticking a hand in the box and rummaging around makes an interesting noise and Amy responds excitedly. We do not specifically choose books for babies or young children, rather we read lots of stories together and she appreciates the rhythm and sounds made. Amy also likes turning the pages and will sometimes want to turn back to the first page. She is also excited by pages with particular colours on them. Reading to the baby is just something I did intuitively.

It is important for parents to get into a routine with their baby. You can advise them that each night before bed it is good to choose a book together; it can be a very simple book with just a few words on a page. Many books are quite tactile with different materials to touch and feel, flaps to lift up or buttons to press. Reading before bed can settle the baby and ensure that there are fewer interruptions during the night. This time together is important. It will help strengthen relationships and help the baby to feel relaxed and safe.

The following conversation between Yolande and her mother illustrates an adult scaffolding learning whilst sharing a book. While Yolande obviously cannot yet talk in full sentences, she is clearly trying to communicate and uses a wide range of sounds to express herself. In holding a proper conversation with the baby, the adult is providing an opportunity to model turn-taking by waiting for the baby's response before continuing. The baby is also learning book handling skills even at this young age. The transcript may read rather strangely but you can see how Mum supports Yolande, and how Yolande is enjoying this book time:

MUM:	It's upside down, look turn it round, turn it round [*the book*]
YOLANDE:	[*Happy scream*]
MUM:	Turn it round
YOLANDE:	Daaaaa
MUM:	If you turn it round it'll be better to see, and you'll be able to see
YOLANDE:	[*Happy scream*]
MUM:	You will
YOLANDE:	[*Happy scream*] – yeh yeh
MUM:	You will
YOLANDE:	Yeh yeh
MUM:	You will
YOLANDE:	Vee yee yee goo goo gee ay yey yey yey
MUM:	Yey yey [*mimicking*], why don't you turn it round then
YOLANDE:	Ooo I yik eee
MUM:	Look I turn it round
YOLANDE:	Do do do do
MUM:	Turn it round, see it's better
YOLANDE:	De de
MUM:	She won't do it, ah – there she has, well done. It's still the wrong way around
YOLANDE:	Dadoo

The following scenario shows the interaction between a father and son. It is extremely important for fathers to read with their children:

MUM:	Adam, Daddy's home
ADAM:	He's here [*screaming with excitement*]
DAD:	Hello chicken. Adam, are you going to read me your book?
ADAM:	Yes sit here
DAD:	Yes, come and sit here with me
ADAM:	Fat Controller [*pointing to his Thomas The Tank Engine book*]. You read it

We will explore reading books with babies further in Chapter 5 and the importance of rhyme, rhythm, sound and song will be discussed in Chapter 6.

Bookstart – Modelling books with babies

Bookstart, run by the national charity Booktrust, was the first national baby book-giving programme in the world. Barrie Wade and Maggie Moore began the idea in 1992 in Birmingham with 300 babies (Wade and Moore, 1998). By 2001 there had been over one million Bookstart babies. Bookstart operates through locally based organisations. The aim is that every child in the UK should enjoy and benefit from books from as early an age as possible and the Bookstart canvas bag is given to parents by their Health Visitor at the 8-month health check. The bag contains baby books, advice booklets for parents on sharing stories, a Sure Start leaflet and an invitation to join the local library.

In an evaluation of Bookstart the National Centre for Research in Childrens Literature (2001) found that Bookstart babies were six times more likely to be library members and their parents were more confident about reading to their children. Some parents may have limited literacy skills, but can be encouraged to look at the pictures with their child and talk about the illustrations. This is beneficial for bonding, giving the child confidence in handling books and starting them on the track of successful reading. The ideal way is for parents to turn off the television, find a comfortable place to read – on a settee, floor, bed or cushions. Books can also be shared in the garden, on a bus, in the car, at the park, in a café and of course at the library, where there is a lot of choice and a child-friendly place to sit and share. Parents are advised that they can buy books at shops and supermarkets, second hand at charity shops or car boot sales, and that books make great presents.

Babies visit libraries

Libraries used to be places where parents dare not take their babies for fear that they would cry or make too much noise. However, many public libraries are now very baby- and child-friendly. There are activities for parents and young children – storytime, singing activity songs and nursery rhymes, and with characterisation and dressing up times with props and toys. The Rainbow Library actively promotes appropriate books that can be chewed and wiped clean – board books, bath books and flannel books.

Libraries can:

- Model and encourage parents to read with babies and young children from an early age
- Provide a welcoming social space for families
- Show that parents are valued and that they are important as their child's first educator
- Provide a variety of materials that can be borrowed, including board books, lift the flap books, videos, DVDs, story sacks
- Create exciting book displays to encourage parents and children to select a range of different books
- Provide activities such as colouring and drawing, story activities, singing, puppets, crafts
- Have story sessions at times to suit parents and carers, including fathers
- Offer dual language story telling sessions and provide dual language books

Babies are readers

Reading stories to children is thought to be *the* most important activity for their success-ful future reading capabilities on entry to school. Gordon Wells's research in the Birmingham literacy projects involved audio-taping the language use in their family lives of 128 young children aged 15 months and then 39 months. The tape recorders were placed in the children's homes and captured the conversations that the children natu-rally engaged in throughout the two and a half years. The results showed that the quality of young children's early language experiences could vary greatly. Jonathan at the age of 4 was shown to experience more than five thousand story experiences with his family, from listening to stories to lots of family conversations where shared experiences occurred and were developed. Rosie, on the other hand, who was a well-cared-for youngest child in a fairly large family, had few 'story' events. The team tracked the chil-dren in their sample as they entered formal schooling and found that the impact of these early 'story' experiences made a difference to the children's capability in school, in their literacy achievements. Jonathan became a star reader whereas Rosie was to experience difficulties with her language use and reading skills.

Parents can be encouraged to:

- Make reading a high priority
- Make it an enjoyable and sharing time
- Involve all members of the family in reading with babies and young children – including siblings and grandparents
- Show that it's important for everyone to read
- Access a wide variety of books – story books, picture books, rhyming books, informa-tion books
- Go to the library on a regular basis
- Be role models through reading for themselves
- Provide quality time for reading
- Read in different places and for different proposes
- Read all print and labelling that surrounds us in the environment
- Buy books for their children
- Involve their children in the selection of books

Watching television, videos and DVDs

Used wisely, television, video or DVD can provide an excellent source of entertainment and be a valuable educational resource for young children. It provides visual and verbal stimuli and can be good for developing communication and extending vocabulary. On the other hand it can also be detrimental to their learning and language acquisition. If it is a passive experience the television cannot respond to the child's questions nor react to their excitement. The following example shows Kaleigh (14 months) and Noel (3 years) watching the *Teletubbies* on television together. Noel is sitting in the chair while Kaleigh is sitting just in front of him. The children act out what they have seen on the television and pretend to share something together as they sing the theme tune and sway from side to side:

NOEL:	Po Isa laa
KALEIGH:	Uh oh
NOEL:	[*carries on singing*]
KALEIGH:	Uh oh
NOEL:	Big hub
KALEIGH:	Gone down
NOEL:	Down, down, down; one for you Ruth, one for Kimberley and two for me
KALEIGH:	Bib bib dada

Recent research has criticised DVDs and videos for babies and young children – that they do not encourage language development, despite marketing claims that they can give a boost. A new study in the USA by Zimmerman and Christakis (2005) found that for every hour per day of watching, young infants may gain fewer words, but there was no difference for toddlers from 17 to 24 months. What is very important is the amount of time spent in front of a screen, whether it is passive or interactive watching, speaking and listening and how rich is the language environment.

After watching *The Lady and the Tramp* video, Jeremy, aged 2, spent the weekend wearing a pyjama collar. He had taken up the message that if you don't wear a collar you'll be taken to the dog pound! This child not only role-played being 'Tramp', but also understood this connotation of 'pound'. The ideal way to use the television as a tool for enhancing a child's language acquisition is for the adult to watch the programme with the child. After the programme has finished, the adult should switch off the television and engage the child in conversation about what they have just watched. It is important to talk about the characters, their names, what they wore, what they were doing etc., and to prompt, encourage responses and get on the same level as the child to talk about what went on. This should be used as an opportunity to spend time together, communicating and getting to know the child's likes and dislikes. It will prove to be a rewarding experience and enhance shared time with the child.

 ## Babies are socialites

Babies who lunch

Six babies aged 12 to 17 months are having lunch together sitting around a table on chairs, strapped in for safety. The children are a social group at lunchtime. They are communicating through observing each other, making eye contact, watching and initiating what is happening, pointing to what they need. There is a lot of language about food and drink promoted by the three practitioners sitting and eating with the children. They eat a lot (at least the children do!) – full plates of pasta and vegetables, feeding themselves using spoons and forks.

Ofsted had been impressed with this excellent practice. No one rushed and everyone had plenty of time in this 'family' situation. The meal was sociable, calm and enjoyable with lots of listening and using language and the toddlers were acquiring independence through the support of the adults and each other.

Parents as partners

Dad and son: rough and tumble rhyme time

Understanding and knowing about the importance of communication definitely can make a difference to how parents interact with their children. Some parents are so keen to promote effective learning for their babies and young children they will find out about theory and read books about language and learning development. *Baby's First Word* is a Talk to Your Baby initiative which encourages parents and carers to talk to and enjoy communicating with their baby. Parents listen out for and report their baby's first word, which is a significant development milestone. A baby's first word shows that he or she is learning sounds and making meaning and wants to communicate this back to you. The Talk to Your Baby initiative advises parents to listen and to try to interpret the words and repeat them back correctly.

Parents can make routine or mundane tasks interesting by talking. For example, when changing a nappy the parent can point out each item of clothing and the baby can then gradually get to know the names of the clothes. The task can be made fun by singing a rhyme together. Here is Lisa's experience:

> Having recently watched the Chatterbox DVD, I realised that the more I interacted with my son, even in everyday mundane tasks, it would enhance our relationship and promote his language and communication skills. So rather than prepare lunch on my own, 14-month-old Tim helped. I brought a chair to the sink for him to stand on and we talked through all the things we needed to do. He helped to wash the lettuce and put it into the colander. He then wanted to help prepare the strawberries. We talked constantly about what we were doing, holding a conversation during this normal household task.

It is important to talk as much as possible with young children, being as equal as possible in the turn-taking. This turn-taking occurs when parents and babies engage with each other in a variety of experiences and activities. Below, we offer some suggestions to help answer some of the parents' most often-asked questions:

1. *I want to teach my baby how to talk properly, should I therefore avoid using baby language such as gurgling and cooing?*
   This is all part of language development. You should mimic your baby as she makes the gurgling and cooing sounds. As you respond to her gurglings, she gets the idea that you want to communicate and you are about to say something. Your approval of the sounds she is making signifies recognition of what she's trying to say and can encourage her to understand words and sounds in her first language more quickly. She also knows that when she makes a sound it will elicit a response. You are rewarding her for her attempts at communicating.

2. *Should I try not to repeat myself? Do I need to think of a new topic of conversation with my baby all the time?*
   Repetition is important. The baby will begin to recognise certain words and, ultimately, these words will become part of his vocabulary. They may even be some of your child's first words.

3. *What should I talk to my baby about?*
   The simple answer is – anything! As you push baby along in the pram, point out the bird sitting on the fence, tell your baby how it is singing a song and talking to the other birds. Now it has flown away into next door's garden. It is going to look for something to eat because it is hungry. Focus on the What? Who? When? Where? Why? questions and make even a simple trip to the local shops interesting by engaging your baby's attention.

 Questions for reflection and discussion

- How can you provide language-rich situations for babies?
- Think about how you can have conversations with babies naturally, without feeling silly.
- Do you recognise features of early language development?
- Do you now feel prepared to answer parents' questions about babies and their language development?

 Key points for practice

- You can't start communicating with babies too early.
- Early experiences are important for brain development.
- Language-rich environments are important.
- Reading to babies is one of the most effective ways of encouraging language.
- Sing songs and rhymes to babies.
- Babies are fun and interesting!.

Further Reading

Forbes, R. (2004) *Beginning to Play: Young Children from Birth to Three.* Maidenhead, Open University Press.

Manning-Morton, J. & Thorpe, M. (2003) *Key Times: The First Three Years.* Maidenhead, Open University Press.

Nutbrown, C. (2006) *Key Concepts in Early Childhood Education and Care.* London, Sage.

Useful websites

www.mumsnet.co.uk
www.literacytrust.org.uk
www.talktoyourbaby.org.uk

Children's Needs: Diversity and Identity

Learning objectives

It is important to understand how children see the world, what their own experiences are and how the language and values of home impact upon their learning. Culture, identity and language are an integral part of children's being – who they are and how they fit into the world. You need to value the diversity of children, their families and the communities in which they live. This is not just for forming effective interactive and warm relationships, but also to capitalise on all aspects of children's knowledge, understanding and experiences. This chapter presents a range of aspects that relate to young children's diversity and identity:

- How to understand and support children's heritage language and emerging bilingualism.
- What gender difference may impact on early language development.
- What special educational needs affect language development.

Supporting children, families and communities

The children you work with will have varied cultural, linguistic, social and economic backgrounds that impact on their early language development, whether they come from indigenous, established or new communities. Culture, identity, knowledge, experience and language are closely interwoven and need to be valued and respected (Brock and Power in Conteh, 2006). Self-esteem, attitudes, social and emotional well-being are important for successful learning to occur. Children may feel devalued if adults do not seem to understand or value what they know and can do. Children must be allowed to be active in the structure of their learning and it is important that they have a wealth of opportunities to be able to co-construct their own understandings and reflect on these with knowledgeable others. It is essential to find out as much as possible about the children you spend time with in order to promote optimum language and learning experiences.

It is important to build strong links and shared understandings between settings and families to enhance young children's social resources and well-being. Parents are the first educators and provide enrichment in the lives of their children, in terms of cultural heritage, religious beliefs and family background and history. You need to build on this expertise and work with parents and carers, recognising and valuing the diversity of ways in which parents support their children at home (Brock and Power in Conteh, 2006). The difference made through empowering families was clearly shown in Bradford's Earlystart Project where outreach workers involved families in play experiences and nursery visits. Families felt that they had important roles to play in their children's early education. You need to listen to and value parents and carers.

Social context and language learning – the role of the adult

The psychologist Vygotsky (1978) suggests that children's language and learning experiences develop through social interaction in cultural contexts, where their learning is guided, modelled and structured by adults or experienced peers. His work on the importance of social context and interaction for children's learning and development is demonstrated through the three levels of:

* Zone of Actual Development (ZAD)
* Zone of Proximal Development (ZPD)
* Zone of Future Development (ZFD)

Vygotsky proposes that children's learning should take place in the 'zone of proximal development', which is the 'zone' or area that is actually just beyond the level of the child's ability to do things independently. Children are supported by knowledgeable others to move from their existing zone of actual development, eventually achieving within their future zone of development. An understanding of children's cultural and language experiences is essential for educators in order for teaching and learning to be most effective. Vygotsky views language as the most powerful cultural tool possessed by young children through which they not only talk and communicate, but also think and internalise their knowledge and understanding. Children organise their knowledge through stories they hear from the adults that surround them.

You need to provide opportunities for children to broaden and deepen their language and learning by providing a variety of first-hand experiences. This can be through talking, storying, singing, drawing, playing, writing or creating models – to name but a few examples.

Language learning through play

Purposeful and practical experiences are extremely important for supporting young children's language and learning. The centrality of play within early years education is therefore key to these discussions. It is what children choose to do, a motivating force that carers and educators need to capitalise on at every opportunity for developing language and learning.

You need to make the most of children's hearing and using language through everyday communication. Providing opportunities for talk is crucial. You need to show children how to use language, how to communicate, how to use dialogue and useful phrases. This is particularly effective when it is done through play. While it may sound complicated, it is a natural process of development. Children need a myriad practical experiences where they speak, listen and interact with others. This is particularly true of young bilingual children, who need activities where they can practise, explore, think and talk aloud as well as opportunities to talk in and beyond practical activities. Children in the early stages of additional language acquisition require thoughtful consideration regarding their particular needs.

Supporting bilingualism

There are immense benefits in supporting bilingualism. Second language acquisition is a complex process and you should make yourself aware of the specific needs of young bilingual children in order to support their language learning (Conteh and Brock, in Conteh, 2006). Most bilingual children in the UK grow up in a predominantly monolingual environment where the first language (or mother tongue) is spoken only in the home with parents, siblings and other relatives. So this language is a major part of their lives, the main conduct of their thought processes. In order for a second language to be truly additional rather than a replacement, the first language needs to be maintained, encouraged and valued (Brock, 1999).

Be aware that young bilingual children may:

- Be very communicative at home and yet reticent in settings
- Use their first language in diverse situations within their families
- Have a good level of understanding of concepts in their first language
- Expect adults to understand them when they use their first language

Code switching

Children in the early stages of acquiring an additional language will often engage in 'code switching' between the first and new language through interspersing the words they know from each language. This supports not only fluency in communication, but also understanding and language learning. Children replace words according to their linguistic expertise and the additional language is actually enhanced. This can be seen in the example below when Wajid, aged 3, interchanges both his languages during a discussion with his Aunty Nusrat. She supports, values and encourages both Wajid's first language of Punjabi and the additional language of English. The conversation takes place some time after Wajid's visit to hospital.

The dialogue shows how fluent Wajid is in Punjabi, how he is learning English and able to switch between the two languages. Notice that Aunty Nusrat scaffolds Wajid's language. They have shared meaning-making and are able to reflect on and discuss their personal history and past experiences. You can learn from conversational analysis – how children use language – and so determine not only what they are saying, but also what they are thinking. Language offers a window into children's minds.

NUSRAT:	Did you stay in hospital?
WAJID:	Yes.
NUSRAT:	Yes. I can remember you went to the hospital.
WAJID:	Chadur, dud, chadur, dud, chadur, dud, chadur [Scarf, milk, scarf, milk, scarf, milk, scarf].
NUSRAT:	Chadur dud, what's that?
WAJID:	You, you, er went to the hospital.
NUSRAT:	I went to the hospital to see you didn't I?
WAJID:	Yes.
NUSRAT:	You had a drip on your arm.
WAJID:	Yes, ai thai see na [Wajid points to his right arm].
NUSRAT:	On your arm.
WAJID:	Yes, I had a teeka, peena nee na sa dud, halley chadur laprey aim see na [Yes I had an injection, couldn't drink the milk, I could only hold the scarf].
NUSRAT:	Kerey chadur? [Which scarf?]
WAJID:	Apni chadur, apni hadur, apni bed a kaul carana na scarf [My scarf, I take it to my bed].
NUSRAT:	Oh yes.
WAJID:	Oh haley laprana sa, dud kol see na laprna karna [I was only holding it, I couldn't hold the milk bottle].
NUSRAT:	I fed you didn't you?
WAJID:	Yes, arhlyaa na sa na Baji, mairay kaul ne bottle laprana, karey karana [Yes, I told you Aunty, I couldn't hold the bottle].
NUSRAT:	Did you like the hospital?
WAJID:	No.
NUSRAT:	Why?
WAJID:	I was poorly, poorly.

As bilingual children develop their language use, they begin to understand that there are two languages being spoken. When Sanela from Slovakia married her English husband and moved to Bradford, she was determined to bring up her children bilingually. Sanela noticed how that clicked into place for her daughter, Sophia, at 2 and a half years old. It happened after Sanela's own mother visited from Slovakia and Sophia realised that there are some books that her grandmother cannot read to her because they are in English and some that she can read because they are in Slovak. Until that point, the mother reasoned that Sophia thought that everybody understood her all the time.

Bilingualism in Wales

The Welsh language provides an example of active government support for encouraging bilingualism. The Welsh Assembly Government is committed to the cause of reviving and revitalising the Welsh language and in 2003 published *Iaith Pawb: a National Action Plan for a Bilingual Wales*.

The Assembly Government attaches great importance to developing Welsh language provision for the early years (0–5 years) and it is seen as an advantage if young children can learn to speak Welsh naturally within the family. For children whose parents do not speak Welsh, Welsh-medium nursery education is seen as a particularly effective means of enabling them to become bilingual. Welsh-medium education for pre-school years is provided in the main by Mudiad Ysgolion Meithrin (MYM) – the Welsh-Medium Nursery Association. This voluntary organisation aims to give every pre-school child in Wales the opportunity to benefit from early years experiences through the medium of Welsh. MYM offers pre-school playgroups or 'nursery circles', (*cylchoedd meithrin*), and '*Ti a Fi*' circles (parent and toddler groups – literally 'You and I circle'). Here parents and guardians can enjoy playing with their children and socialising in an informal Welsh atmosphere and non-Welsh speaking parents can learn Welsh alongside their children.

Supporting bilingual children in educational settings

Supporting first and additional language is important for developing young children's thinking, understanding and learning. Meaningful, communicative situations where they can practise both their languages are therefore crucial otherwise 'semilingualism' can occur. This is when a child fails to acquire the first language to the same standard as would be anticipated in a monolingual child, and the child might not achieve a higher level of capability in either language. You need to develop your own understanding of supporting and developing first and additional language; make opportunities to monitor young bilingual children's language development and also provide a multitude of experiences and activities where young children use language. On playing a short audio tape recording of the story of Winnie the Pooh in Japanese, it was interesting to note how many people stopped listening and switched off within a matter of seconds. They simply didn't understand. Think about putting yourself in the same position of not having a 'comprehensible input' – and ask yourself how long you will stay the course if you don't understand any of the words!

On learning an additional language, children may at first opt out of talking and engage in a period of silence because they may:

- Not understand every word
- Not feel confident to express themselves
- Know they are not fluent in an additional language
- Feel pressurised or inhibited
- Have difficulty following long sentences
- Lack the necessary vocabulary to identify objects and events

It is important that you are aware of these factors and foster a positive attitude towards supporting bilingualism.

Your role in supporting the bilingual child

- Be aware of how you use language
- Model language that children can imitate
- Match language to activities and experiences
- Repeat vocabulary very regularly in meaningful situations

- Ensure children understand the vocabulary
- Allow time for children to think, consolidate and translate
- Connect first language to additional language
- Encourage and praise to promote self-confidence

In order to do these effectively you need to provide a wealth of experiences that:

- Promote a lot of opportunities for children to talk
- Consolidate language and meaning
- Offer exciting, stimulating and meaningful activities
- Make learning fun
- Promote learning through play, first-hand and active experiences
- Support learning through practical resources, visual support and other children

The following is a practical example of how to support young children's bilingualism through an interpretation of the story of the 'Three Billy Goats Gruff' (renamed as 'Bruffs' in this personalised edition). Everyone, or nearly everyone, knows this traditional story. It is a super story because it is repetitive, full of movement, about animals and has heroes and a villain! Children love stories (see more in Chapter 5) and this particular story can be explored in innumerable ways. It can be told in first and additional language through reading aloud, on audio-tape, video or through role-play, drama, or a PowerPoint presentation. The latter method, along with an audio recording in Hindu/Urdu, was used with bilingual children in a foundation stage setting, both to support understanding and to demonstrate that their first language was valued.

A story is a brilliant way to encourage additional language learning through illustrations, repetition and rhythm. This is particularly so if there is code switching to help cue children into the additional language. See an excerpt from the story on page 48, which has photographs, English text and transliteration of Hindu/Urdu. Why not photocopy the page, cut out the sentences and have a go at matching the phonetically translated sentence strips to the English? Teaching students in England and delegates at an international conference in Florida accomplished this successfully and were soon 'storytelling' in Hindu/Urdu. Work collaboratively if you can, so you can discuss it. Put yourself into the experience of being a new language learner. What are the difficulties? What helps you to learn most effectively? How can you build on this experience and develop your understanding of children learning an additional language?

Children should engage with the story many times and in many different ways – through role-play with masks; puppets, playscapes and story sacks. See Brock and Power's chapter in Conteh (2006) for further practical ideas for supporting language and learning. It is a good idea to allow children with the same first language to work together in both languages, to encourage bilingualism.

Supporting bilingualism at home

English needs to be an additional language and should not replace children's first language. Once English is reasonably well established, teachers in schools are rarely encouraged to support bilingual development using the heritage or first language. Families usually want their children to be fluent enough in English to be successful at school, but whether they are able also to maintain equal proficiency in the original language can vary greatly. One major advantage of encouraging young children to master more than one language is that bilinguals acquire an ability to translate and label concepts in different ways. The fact that they are not restricted to one way of viewing the world makes learning additional languages later in life much easier.

 A bilingual child: Sanela, aged 2 years 5 months

Sanela highlights the challenge of trying to bring up children bilingually. Living in England and being completely surrounded by English language culture means that although her family visits a few times a year, there is insufficient opportunity for Sophia to hear or speak Slovak. To encourage language acquisition, the mother and daughter read Slovakian books together. However, Sanela points out that compared with English books, they are not as attractive to look at and handle and are usually English books or foreign language books translated into Slovak so the language does not flow as well. The mother explains certain games or activities in Slovakian and Sophia knows the body parts as part of the bath routine. She knows the names of certain animals in Slovakian and can count up to 14 since there are 14 stairs in the house and they count them together as they walk down. She also knows the colours and the names of every day items that they either play with or use, such as the kitchen utensils through emptying the dishwasher together. However her Slovakian is nowhere near as fluent as her English and while she can understand Slovakian and has a good vocabulary, she does not speak it as naturally as English and usually responds in English.

Gender and identity

Gender identities are brought out through language, personal experience, activities and interaction with others. Children's ability to co-construct and negotiate their positions through language has implications for their achievement in schools, and ultimately their successful participation in society. Watch children when they are engaged in outdoor play activities. Are boys more physically dominant? Do girls build a sense of community in their language? Research shows that both genders can vie for position, boys for dominance, girls to be the nicest (Kyratzis, 2001; Jarvis, 2006). Girls are more likely to use mitigating language to smooth squabbles in a group. Play, rough and tumble games and dialogue with other children are all vital elements, which enable children to discover themselves, their role and position within the group. Some researchers propose that boys engaging in rough and tumble forms the basis for male socialisation and helps develop skills for later rule-based sporting activities and language-based competition (Jarvis, 2006).

Opportunities for free play are therefore vitally important. Most boys love to run, fight, jump and play. On taking his boys on a trip to the Bretton Country Park, one father remarked on how much the boys loved just running around in the wide open space, down through the long grass and across the green meadows. They needed opportunity to let off steam and expend energy. Another example is when Akram, Johnny, Kevin and Rhys were working collaboratively at the kitchen table to make a 'Lord of the Rings' playscape. It was exciting to see how well the boys responded to instructions, how their imaginative thinking grew and how they helped to further develop each other's ideas.

Promoting self-esteem and positive behaviour through language

Language therefore has an important role in socialisation and forming relationships. Children need to know how to use language in many and varied situations. Young children have to learn to control their emotions and learn to communicate with their peers, siblings and adults in society. They need the wherewithal and support of adults in order to cope effectively. This is hard when you are very young and you want your needs met immediately! You just have to have the toy that your friend is holding at the moment, you don't particularly want to share, and you need it now. Turn taking, sharing, responding and listening to others has to be learnt.

Conflict resolution

High/Scope have produced a very useful video on conflict resolution that offers practitioners a strategy to support young children. It demonstrates how to provide children with effective language to cope in fraught situations. Conflict resolution can be very time-consuming, but the results pay off. Time is required to listen to the children, to support them and facilitate their understanding and communication. In the video, the practitioner translates and code switches between Spanish and English, so time was also needed to translate into the languages that the children understood. The children were obviously used to listening to more than one language and on the video you can see the quality of their listening. At the beginning of an argument about a set of keys, the three children involved are extremely upset and even angry. The little boy has snatched the keys and really wants them. The girls are equally upset to have had the keys taken away. The conflict has to be resolved and the practitioner is determined that the children have to be helped to negotiate and come to a conclusion that is accepted by all parties. He is very patient and takes the time needed for this process to be worked through.

High/Scope nurseries in the UK also practise this. At one West Yorkshire setting Susan was sitting on the floor with two children who had had a slight altercation in the rough and tumble playroom. All three were reflecting on the incident and talking it through. Everyone's opinion was listened to and valued. Susan:

- Modelled not only good behaviour, but also listening skills
- Ensured the children had time to think things through and talk about them
- Encouraged self-expression (knowing how to talk about the incidents and confident that the adult will listen)
- Listened (appreciating other's points of view)
- Encouraged discussion (participating in discussion that ensures active listening in others, not just expressing one's point of view)
- Ensured a resolution (enabling the children involved to come to an agreement)

Communication difficulties

Children may have tantrums because they cannot communicate effectively or feel that adults do not understand them. This can be caused by communication and language difficulties, and exploring the quality of their hearing or eyesight can make a huge difference. Nicky was diagnosed as having a hearing problem at 18 months, which although it affected his pronunciation and speech development, he was a cheerful, playful child and full of fun. However, two years later he became miserable, unresponsive and disruptive, throwing tantrums and exhibiting anti-social behaviour. A further hearing check and visit to the specialists with the fitting of grommets restored Nicky to his former happy and communicative self.

Language delay

In 2002 the Basic Skills agency found that 50 per cent of children starting school lack vital communication and language skills. Locke et al. (2002) reported that early years practitioners were stating that many children, in particular from disadvantaged social and economic families, were entering settings without the necessary spoken language skills needed to develop literacy. They also found it was also more likely to be boys than girls. It is therefore crucial that your setting becomes a language-rich environment that makes early language and communication a high priority, especially for those disadvantaged children who are at risk of language delay (Potter, 2007).

Language delay can be connected to maturation and be a part of a child's individual developmental process. Issues should be discussed with parents, whilst being careful not to cause worry. Information-sharing and regular observation in settings, at home and in different situations is crucial. Observe children playing and communicating both indoors and outdoors, in the sand tray, water trough, large construction, role-play area, at story and circle time to see if there are differences. Often young children with poor communication skills can show rapid improvement when in an environment that encourages the need to communicate with other children and adults. Play experiences with interested adults can provide motivation and stimulation to develop language. However, a move into a new setting can unsettle children who may feel insecure with unfamiliar people and places and become withdrawn, silent or shy. Patience is obviously a key strategy in supporting transition. It is good practice to:

- Become rapidly aware of children's individual needs
- Discover their interests
- Establish structured routines
- Encourage familiarity with the environment
- Form open and warm relationships with young children and their families
- Create a working partnership through two-way communication with parents
- Continually share and request information

Supporting special educational needs

Whilst this section does not offer in-depth guidance about special needs, it draws attention to the range of difficulties children may have in connection with communication and language. It provides some information on what to look for and offers advice on how to support young children and their families. There will also be guidance as to where to seek further information, advice and ideas.

The DfES definition of SEN is the official term applied to children in the UK who are identified as having difficulties that may require additional support or provision to ensure they reach their potential. Each of the features related to language development – phonology, grammar, syntax, semantics and pragmatics – has conditions that impinge on their effectiveness. A speech and language impairment is normally characterised by the late appearance of comprehension and expression.

- Receptive language is the understanding of what others say and do: listening, following instructions, memory.
- Expressive language is being able to use words, gestures, movements, tone and expressions so that others can understand: speech, vocabulary, grammar and syntax.

Where there are concerns about a child's language development, it is important to seek advice from a speech and language therapist (SLT). Many children's centres (and some schools) now have either a resident or visiting SLT and many settings work in multi-agency teams. If this is not the case then contact local authority services which will put you in touch with the right sort of help. Observation, monitoring and recording are essential to provide detail that can show patterns or instances that can indicate problems and provide evidence to be analysed.

Practitioner's communicative role

- Think about language use, length of sentences, specific vocabulary
- Allow time for children: for listening, for speaking and for doing
- Use gesture and movement
- Emphasise intonation and voice expression
- Stress vocabulary and/or use onomatopoeic language, e.g. in the water tray: pour, splash, drip, plop, swish
- Interpret what children mean, which may be different from what children say
- Check children's understanding: through questions, seeing if they can follow instructions, but mainly through observing what they are doing and how they are responding to activities, other adults and children
- Set manageable tasks and have reasonable expectations
- Offer praise and encouragement
- Ask questions where children have to say a word. Do you want juice or milk?
- Be informed through finding out more about any specific disorders
- Learn Makaton and/or simple signing and involve all children.

Supportive experiences and activities

- Be aware of the environment – the amount of light, noise, space etc.
- Be interactive through using resources and contextualising activities
- Use alternative means of communication: signs, symbols, large print
- Use information and communication technology: computers, audio tapes, switches
- Promote multisensory experiences, emphasising smell, touch, sight and sound as appropriate

- Provide opportunities for large physical play and gross motor movement
- Pass round physical resources in circle time to support language
- Allow children to express themselves in different ways: through rhythm, song, dance, gross motor movement, painting, modelling, construction, sculpting, hammering
- Play simple repetitive games
- Sing songs and rhymes that have actions and movement
- Share interactive books that have flaps, pop-ups or are multisensory
- Tell stories with gestures, movement, lots of intonation and stress
- Get children's attention – good listening, good sitting, good looking, good thinking and good turn-taking are often used as a behavioural technique, but are valuable ways of establishing clear communication strategies

Here are two case studies of children who had particular difficulties with communication and language. They demonstrate how families coped with these challenging situations and the positive outcomes for the children.

 A child with hearing impairment: Ivor, age 13 months

Ivor failed his neonatal hearing test when he was one day old, which is not uncommon. However, when he failed again four weeks later and again at six months, his mum was convinced he was totally deaf. The hospital specialists later confirmed that Ivor was deaf in both ears and he has been referred for cochlea implants to be fitted when he is 18 months old. The remarkable thing about this family is that in order to be able to learn to communicate with Ivor, not only mum, but the extended family attended classes to learn how to use sign language. Ivor's older siblings even take part in signing lessons at school. The siblings are proud of their younger brother. They show him off to their friends and shout in Ivor's ears to show them he's deaf. Ivor himself copies the signs and now at 13 months can understand ten signs and perform six, including drink, eat, ball, bird and light. As with hearing children, who start to talk a word at a time, the same is true of signing: it begins slowly and then escalates. Although Ivor has hearing aids, he pulls them out at playgroup when his mother is not looking! The family engages in lots of talk with Ivor, so he can also begin to lip read.

 A child who was an elective mute for a time: Evan, age 6

Evan was 18 months old when he came to us as our foster-adoptive child. He had had a rough time, in and out of care. There were suggestions of abuse, so he was very stressed. He had settled with his foster parents, but then when he came to us, and met Robbie, an articulate 3-year-old who would be his older brother, Evan just shut down. It was as though a brick wall had come between us and him; he would sit there looking from behind this wall, withdrawn into himself. The first week or two he cried a lot, he wouldn't settle, having bad dreams through the night. Then, after two weeks he stopped crying noisily, there were just tears and no sounds. He had been using single words, like juice, with his foster parents, but he stopped talking altogether. It might have been the presence of Robbie, who was rather precocious and would do the talking for him, but Evan didn't seem to gain in his language; he could understand but wouldn't talk. Apparently he had been strapped into his baby buggy a lot and left to sit and he would stay sitting and passive for hours and hours. It didn't help that he had to have a series of operations, skin grafts, and then had an iron deficiency. After this, when the treatment was finished and he had spent a long time with us, he started to relax more. At the age of 3 he started talking quite fluently in full sentences. Evan started school a term early and initially liked his first teacher, but then he started to become mute again at school. He talked at home, but refused to at school. This continued for some time until he was 6-years-old when a new child entered school from another county, who became very distressed and also refused to speak. Evan took him under his wing, they started communicating and Evan started translating for him. By the end of that year both boys were talking competently.

You need to be aware that there is a number of conditions that can affect communication and language including Asperger's syndrome, auditory processing difficulties, autistic spectrum disorders, cleft palate, echolalia, hearing impairment and lisp. It is not possible for you to have expert knowledge about all these conditions. This chapter will have alerted you to a variety of children's individual needs and offered some ideas of what to look for and how to support these children. When you encounter a particular need, you will have to find out more to support your practice. This means talking to the child, parents and family, colleagues and other professionals. It will also mean that you will have to do some further research and reading. A good place to start is I CAN, the national education charity for children with speech and language difficulties. The I CAN Talking Point website provides information about communication, development and disability. It has a library of publications, factsheets, products and resources. The focus is on supporting children with a communication disability and provides a combination of specialist therapy and education for children with the most severe and complex disabilities, information for parents and training and advice for teachers and other professionals. You should also refer to the National Association for Special Educational Needs (NASEN), which aims to promote the education, training, advancement and development of all those who work with children with special educational needs.

 Questions for reflection and discussion

- Are you aware of individual children's culture, identity and language?
- Why do you think it is important to support children's bilingualism?
- Consider what differences there might be between boys and girls acquiring and using language.
- How do all these affect your practice?

Key points for practice

- Supporting culture, language and identity is important.
- Children need a myriad practical experiences.
- First language should be maintained, encouraged and valued.
- Gender and identity may have impact on language and communication.
- Developing your knowledge and getting professional advice is important for supporting SEN.

 Further Reading

Conteh, J. (ed.) (2006) *Promoting Learning for Bilingual Pupils 3–11*. London: Sage.

Jones, C.A. (2004) *Supporting Inclusion in the Early Years*. Maidenhead: Open University Press.

Thompson, G. (2003) *Supporting Children with Communication Disorders*. London: David Fulton.

 Useful websites

www.talkingpoint.org.uk
http://fabula.mozdev.org
www.actionaid.org.uk
www.standardsdfes.gov.uk/ethnicminorities
www.icon.org.uk
http://www.nasen.org.uk/

This is Big Billy Goat Bruff.

Ek toe burah bukri ta.

This is Middle Size Billy Goat Gruff.

Ek toe beachwala bukri ta.

This is Little Billy Goat Bruff.

Ek toe chotiwla bukri ta.

They lived in a field but the field had no grass.

Ek medan meh rehtee tay lakin ek medan meh grass nahi ta.

A bridge was nearby. A troll lived under the bridge.

Ek bridge kepas ta. Ek troll bridge meinrehtata

Trip trap trip trap.

Trip trap trip trap.

Billy Goats Bruff activity

Communication, Language and Literacy from Birth to Five SAGE © 2008
Avril Brock and Carolynn Rankin

4

Getting Young Children Talking in Early Years Settings

Carol Potter

 Learning objectives

This chapter is about the importance of creating high-quality opportunities for communication between adults and young children in early years settings. It will inform you of why it is necessary to encourage young children to take the lead in conversations. You will find out about taking the role of facilitator rather than director in children's play. Adults need to create effective opportunities for communication using a range of strategies, including the use of pausing and asking the right kind of questions. You therefore need to be very aware of the role you play, both in your provision and how you use language; the environment, activities and how to support young children in their language learning are crucial. The chapter looks at:

- How to promote sustained shared thinking
- How to develop good communication opportunities when talking with one child and also when working with a group
- The importance of working closely with parents regarding their child's communication.

This chapter has two main messages: the first is that the ways in which we talk with young children have an enormous effect on how their language and communication develop as they grow older. Some of the ways in which we talk with them are more beneficial than others and we will look at this in some detail.

The second thing to emphasise is that although we know that it's very important for children to have many opportunities for prolonged conversations with adults in early years settings, you may be aware that it is often a struggle to make time for this to happen on a daily basis. You probably have good ideas as to why this is the case. One of the biggest reasons is to do with staffing ratios. As you will know, there is usually only one adult for every four or five young children in early years settings and this obviously affects how much time there is to talk to each child. You will also be aware that there is a number of important tasks to be carried out each day – for example, filling in records, liaising with parents and preparing activities – which affect the amount of time you have to spend talking directly with children. This is an issue we will go on to discuss later in the chapter, giving practical suggestions for how you can create as many communication opportunities as possible in your settings, given the constraints on your time.

Getting children to start conversations

Let's start then by looking at how you, as adults in early years settings, talk with children. It's not just a matter of how *often* you interact with children that makes a difference, it is also important to look closely at who does what in the conversation. In an important piece of research, Gordon Wells (1987) found that staff in school settings began many more conversational turns with children than parents did at home. In other words, children led more conversations at home than in school. More recently, when Potter and Hodgson (2007) analysed some tape-recorded conversations between nursery nurses and children, they found that staff began two-thirds of all conversational turns. Such findings are worrying because we know that for children to become better communicators, it is very important that they have frequent experience of starting conversations. This is because when children take the lead, they are likely to talk more and use their language more creatively than if they are simply responding to what we, as adults, have said. For this to happen, we must work towards children starting more conversational turns much more often.

If children have experience of only *responding* to what we, as adults, say in their early years, their language may not develop as well as it could. So how can you help children to start more conversations with you? The first thing is to find out what is happening now in your setting, by asking the following questions:

- When you talk with children, who starts the conversation?
- How often do you, as adults, start a conversational turn?
- How often do the children start the conversation?

This can be a more difficult task than it sounds for a number of reasons. As adults and competent communicators, we use thousands of words each day and it is hard to step back and think critically about what we are actually saying and how we use our speech. There are, however, two good ways of finding out about how we use speech in everyday settings.

The easiest way to find out who is starting conversations in your setting is to take some video tape of yourself talking with one child, perhaps for a five-minute period. When reviewing the tape or DVD afterwards, you will be able to see more clearly who is leading each conversational turn. If you discover that you or other adults are leading most of the turns then you will need to think about how you can change this pattern, and to do this you will need to consider how you are prompting children's talk, which we are going to look at next.

Consider the following short interaction, which was video-taped between a nursery nurse and a 4-year-old child:

ADULT:	What colour are the stripes?
CHILD:	Him got paws
ADULT:	Has he?
CHILD:	Yeah they got paws
ADULT:	Has it?
CHILD:	Doggie
ADULT:	Doggie? It's got paws?
CHILD:	Yeah
ADULT:	What have you got down there?
	What have you got down there?
CHILD:	Only socks
ADULT:	Only socks?
CHILD:	They not Simon's – they mine.
ADULT:	They're not Simon's?
	Do you wear Simon's sometimes?
CHILD:	Yeah.
ADULT:	Do you?
	Where's Simon today?
CHILD:	I don't know

The adult here asks 12 questions during a one-minute interaction, leading each turn in the conversation. The child concerned replies with only one-, two- or three-word phrases throughout. How did this happen? If we look carefully at what was going on in the conversation, we can see that the nursery nurse was using only questions to prompt the child to talk and this meant that the child could only respond. From your own experience, you might be aware that this kind of conversation is very common in early years settings, perhaps because you as staff may not have received enough training on other ways of getting children talking. How we prompt young children to talk is a very important one because the kind of prompts we use go a long way to determining whether children start conversations or adults do.

Prompting children's talk

How we prompt children to talk is important. What do we mean by prompting? Putting it simply, a prompt is anything an adult says or does to encourage a child to speak. In pre-school settings, you will use hundreds of prompts every day in your work with children. It is very important for you to try to become aware of the kind of prompts you are using because some will result in better learning opportunities for children than others.

How we use questions

As we saw above, one of the most frequent types of prompt we use with children is questions. What Gordon Wells (1987) found by tape-recording children talking at and in school was that staff in schools asked many more questions than parents did at home. The important thing to note here is *that questions are almost always conversation starters*. If you ask a lot of questions, as an adult in an early years setting, you will almost certainly be starting a lot of conversational turns, which as we saw above, is not necessarily the most helpful strategy for developing children's language.

For our purposes, there are two main types of questions, closed and open. Generally, the least helpful type of question is a closed one, the answer to which can be only one or two words. Open questions give the child greater scope for a longer reply. Figure 4.1 gives you a list of these different types of question words.

Closed questions (least useful)	Open questions (most useful)
What?	Why?
Who?	How?
Which?	
Where?	
How many?	

Figure 4.1 Different types of question words

The least useful question words are generally 'What', 'Where' and 'Who' because they usually require a short factual response. The other kinds of questions we often use with children are tag questions, where we repeat what a child has just said and then add a question to it, as we see below:

> CHILD: I'm drawing a house.
> ADULT: You're drawing a house, *are you*?
> CHILD: That's blue.
> ADULT: That's blue, *is it*?

The problem with tag questions is that they are *closed questions*, requiring a one-word answer at best. Question words which are much more useful are 'Why' and 'How' because they generally require a longer and more complex response from children. For example:

> ADULT: How did you make that house?
> CHILD: Well, I got some Lego and I put this red piece onto that blue piece ... then I put more and more bricks on to make the walls.

If we, as adults, use only closed questions, then children will have practice in producing only short one- or two-word phrases in response, rather than longer more complex ones. We need to work on asking children many more open questions of the 'how' and 'why' variety to help them develop their language skills.

Practice ideas

So, having explained what the issues are around asking questions, you might well ask what you can do about it. The first thing to do is to find out how many questions you are currently using, by asking:

- What kind of questions do we use now?
- How often do we use them?
- What kind of questions are they?

Take five minutes of video tape of staff working with one child with an activity the child has chosen. Review the tape and count how many questions there are and what kind of questions they are. Staff could observe each other for five minutes in the same situation and count how many questions are asked.

Using such an approach can be an eye-opener. This is what one nursery nurse said after watching herself talking with a young child:

> I mean if someone had said – 'You talk too much and ask loads of questions' – I would have thought 'Oh do I?' I would have probably thought 'No – I don't think I do really' you know … but actually watching it and seeing yourself – you think …'Why have I asked that many questions – just questioned them and questioned them – interrupted their talk and not given them time?' – when you see the video you can actually see it's what you're doing.

In the area of questions, you need to be working towards

- Asking fewer questions
- Asking fewer closed questions (What, Where, Which, Who)
- Using more open questions (How did you, Why did you)

You may well be wondering how you can change this pattern of asking lots of questions. Don't worry! There are some quite straightforward ways of cutting down on the number of questions you ask, at the same time as getting children to start more conversations – as we shall see below.

Pausing: let the silence do the work!

Using more pauses when talking with young children is one of the most effective ways of reducing the number of questions you ask, whilst at the same time allowing children to take a greater lead in conversations.

Although pauses are a natural part of everyday conversations, we, as adults are very sensitive to their length. Because most of us are able to talk freely and fluently, any pause that lasts longer than a few seconds makes us feel uneasy and embarrassed. Therefore, when we are talking to children and silences develop, we often feel compelled to fill them, often with questions.

We need to learn to use longer pauses with children because children need more time to think about what they have heard and to find the words they will need to reply or begin a new turn in the conversation. Children who experience any kind of language difficulties will need even more time to produce speech and so adults may need to wait even longer. Again, the use of video tape is very useful here.

The conversation below shows how a nursery nurse uses a number of pauses to encourage a child to take the lead in the interaction:

> CHILD: I'm not finished yet.
> ADULT: No I'm not finished either – I think I'll do a ... [*pause*]
> CHILD: Spider!
> ADULT: A spider! ... [*pause*]
> ADULT: Oh that's a good idea ... [*pause*]
> ADULT: He's going to be a wiggly spider
> CHILD: I know what that is
> ADULT: Well done ... [*pause*] ... Oh I see you're cutting out some red [*pause*]
> CHILD: Black
> ADULT: Ooohhh ... [*pause*]
> CHILD: Rip it off [*as he does so – sticks paper on card*] I'm not finished yet
> ADULT: No – I can see that ... [*pause*]
> CHILD: Do you know what it is?
> ADULT: I don't – not yet ... [*pause*]
> CHILD: I haven't finished – I might make a snowball fight.
> ADULT: Wow – lots of snow!

By pausing after each of her turns in the conversation, the nursery nurse constantly hands back the initiative to the child she is talking to and interestingly the child is able to accept the opportunity. Each pause the adult introduces allows the child to consider what he may say next and to think about and produce the speech. Throughout the interaction, the child initiates each turn: he is getting very good experience of leading a conversation.

Changing the adult's role: from director to facilitator

Another important approach to consider when encouraging children's talk is your role as the adult in the conversation. We have seen how easy it is for us, as adults, in pre-school settings, to become questioners rather than facilitators. There will certainly be times when you will need to direct children's activity during transition times or at the end of sessions but your role during activities can be significantly changed in such a way as to encourage more child-led talk. Let's look below at how this can be done.

Practice ideas

Rather than directing children's activities, you as an adult, can play alongside children, engaging in the activity yourself as a participant. Within such a scenario, the dynamics of the conversation change quite significantly with a number of spin-offs. To begin with, there is less pressure on children to speak since your focus of attention is partly on your own activity. In addition, your own actions generate a source of interest for the children, which may also prompt some speech. Consider the following extract in which Hannah, a nursery nurse, is herself painting alongside a small group of children.

	Speech	**Type of adult prompt**
HANNAH:	Backwards and forwards, Nathan, brush, brush, brush … [*pause*]	**Comment** on own activity and **pause**
DAVID:	What what are you making? [*to Hannah*]	
HANNAH:	I'm painting a flower … [*pause*] [*children laugh*]	**Reply** and **pause**
HANNAH:	Nice red petals … [*pause*]	**Comment** on own activity
DAVID:	What what what's that?	
HANNAH:	That's the leaf … [*children laugh*]	**Reply** and **pause**
JOHN:	That's the sun [*putting orange blob on Hannah's picture*]	
HANNAH:	Oooh, thank you – that's nice and bright … [*pause*]	**Reply, comment** and **pause**

During this conversation, we see that the member of staff is engaged in painting her own picture. At the start of the conversation, she draws attention to what she is doing by talking about it in an enthusiastic way and then pausing. Her attempt to prompt child talk is successful because David then asks her about what she is doing. It is clear that the children are interested and amused by Hannah's painting, going on to ask further questions. Then one of the children, John, decides to contribute to Hannah's picture, adding a sun and commenting on what he is doing. In this short interaction, the member of staff has skilfully managed to reverse the often witnessed 'adult question/child reply' scenario. Here, the children are asking the questions and leading the interaction. As well as enabling children to lead the talk, Hannah has also introduced several new words, in an attempt to develop the children's vocabulary: 'backwards', 'forwards', 'leaf', 'petal' and 'bright'. In summary, the approaches this nursery nurse has successfully used to facilitate children talking are:

- Playing alongside with enthusiasm
- Using comments, pauses, replies (not questions)
- Introducing new words into the activity to extend vocabulary

In fact, extending children's vocabulary is another vital area to consider in the development of young children's language and we will explore key issues and how to address them in the next section.

Building vocabularies

There is one key finding from research which is very important for everyone working with young children to understand. This is that:

- The number of words that children know and can use is the best predictor of later reading success.

Why should this be the case? A large part of the answer is that when children are in the early stages of sounding out words, they are much more likely to make correct guesses when the printed words in question are ones they already know and use. In this way, children with larger vocabularies are more likely to make more successful guesses and so make a much better start to decoding print. They experience success more often than children with limited vocabularies and become more confident in their reading abilities.

Practical ideas

So then, how can you best build children's vocabularies in pre-school settings? You need to try to introduce new words regularly and reinforce them in a number of situations so that children absorb them and then begin to use the new vocabulary themselves. It is a matter of extending what children say by adding new words consistently within conversations:

Example 1
CHILD: It's a bus.
ADULT: Yes, it's a big, red bus.

Example 2
CHILD: I've got lots of play-dough.
ADULT: Yes, it's very sticky and soft.

This will be what you are most likely already trying to do all of the time. But did you know that young children may need to hear a new word up to 500 times before they begin to use it themselves? With this important fact in mind, it becomes clear that you need to have quite a structured way of making sure that everyone in your setting is introducing roughly the same new words and ideas, so that children get the maximum number of chances of hearing them and so that they can eventually go on to use them.

Possible problems: finding the words

One of the possible difficulties staff may initially experience when attempting to introduce new vocabulary is bringing to mind a sufficiently wide range of new words whilst in the act of supporting children within activities. As you know, there is a lot to do in terms of helping and encouraging young children in any activity, and, understandably, it can be very hard whilst 'in the thick of it' to bring to mind new vocabulary. This can sometimes lead to the introduction of only a limited selection of new words.

Possible solutions: word lists

To overcome this real difficulty, you could think about producing laminated lists of relevant vocabulary for a range of activities to have at hand. These could be extended to relate to changing topics over the year. The main advantages of having such lists are that they:

- Can be thought out beforehand so that a wider range of vocabulary has been identified
- The target vocabulary is readily available to all staff engaged in a particular activity
- Different staff leading the same activity will be introducing the same vocabulary, making it more likely that children will absorb the new words

Different types of words could be identified within the lists to ensure that children are developing different aspects of their vocabularies, for example: object names (nouns); describing words (adjectives); action words (verbs).

For example, extended vocabulary lists could be developed for the following activities:

- Playing with cars
- Computer
- Construction
- Painting
- Baking
- Outside play
- Snack time
- Musical instruments
- Role play
- Sand and water play
- Board games

Sometimes it can be especially hard to bring to mind new vocabulary in areas such as car play or when using board games, it can be easy to fall back on the same kinds of words. When considering car play and computers, a vocabulary list might include the words shown in Figure 4.2 and 4.3 respectively.

Increasing the number of communication opportunities

We have talked about how you as adults in pre-school settings can help children to become starters of conversations as well as how you can build up their vocabularies in more structured ways. We will now turn to how you can increase the number of communication opportunities you can offer children. As we discussed above, you will probably be well aware that one of the biggest obstacles to providing frequent communication opportunities for each and every child in any pre-school setting is the staffing ratio. At its simplest, the problem is that one adult can interact directly with only one child at a time which has a significant effect on the number of communication opportunities that can be offered. A key question for staff in early years settings is:

- How many high quality opportunities for communication does each child have during a nursery session?

Word	Type of word	Word	Type of word	Word	Type of word
Tyres	Object words: (Nouns)	Accelerating	Action words: (Verbs)	Gleaming	Describing words: (Adjectives)
Bonnet		Slowing		Bright	
Sun roof		Braking		Dull	
Windscreen		Indicating		Scratched	
Indicators		Overtaking		Adjustable	

Figure 4.2 Example of word list: playing with cars

Word	Type of word	Word	Type of word	Word	Type of word
Mouse	Object words: (Nouns)	Pushing	Action words: (Verbs)	Square	Describing words: (Adjectives)
Screen		Clicking		Sharp	
Key board		Accessing		Blurred	
Space bar		Scrolling		Clear	
Programme		Printing		Silver	

Figure 4.3 Example of word list: computers

Working with large groups

Practice ideas

There is a number of straightforward ways you can think about increasing the number of communication opportunities offered within your settings. One of the most important areas to start thinking about is how much time children spend in large group situations, such as listening to stories or taking part in musical activities. Whilst it is certainly important that young children learn how to take part in such groups, it is also vital to think about communication opportunities on offer in such scenarios. In fact, each child in a large group session may have only one chance to speak in a 15-minute period, simply because you, as the adult, may be managing a session with between 15 and 20 children.

Furthermore, if you observe a few of your large group sessions from the point of view of the communication opportunities they provide for children, you may find that not only is the frequency of such occurrences low but they are also likely to be fairly brief. This is understandable because in order to maintain order within large groups of young children, you will probably find yourself having to be quite directive, which usually involves asking closed questions to which children will generally give one- or two-word replies. You will also be aware that there is generally little opportunity for sustained shared thinking with individual children in large groups since you, as the adult leading the session, want to both maintain the interest of all of the children and give others the chance to speak.

The other issue here is that very often, whilst you are leading the session, one or two other members of staff may be observing or trying to maintain children's attention. You might reflect that perhaps the time of these other two members of staff could be used more effectively.

So, let's think about this. To find out what is going on in your setting regarding large group work, you might find it useful to ask yourselves the following questions:

* How much time do children in your setting spend in large groups each day?
* How many opportunities for communication does each child have during large group sessions?
* What kind of opportunities are they?

After you have thought about these issues, you may want to think again about the balance of time spent between large and small group work as well as time spent with individual children. Let's think about how you might begin to adapt some traditionally large group sessions to try to increase the number of communication opportunities available for each child.

Sustained shared thinking

In the section above I mentioned 'sustained shared thinking' (SST). Let's take a moment to think about what this is and why it is important. Researchers talked about this idea during their work on the important EPPE project (Effective Provision of Pre-School Education). This project followed the progress of 3,000 children from entering pre-school to the end of Key Stage 2. The children all attended different kinds of pre-school provision and the project wanted to find out which aspects of provision made a difference to children's development. They found that children in pre-school environments that encourage 'sustained shared thinking' between adults and children make better progress than children in settings that do not. Professor Iram Siraj-Blatchford, who led the EPPE project, said that sustained shared thinking is where staff 'actively teach the children, which means modelling appropriate language and behaviour, sharing intelligent conversations, asking questions and using play to motivate and encourage them.' (Siraj-Blatchford et al, 2002).

Take a look at the conversation below, which gives an example of an adult and child involved in some sustained shared thinking.

JAMES:	I can't get my tower to stand up –
ADULT:	It keeps falling down.
JAMES:	Yeah – it gets wobbly and crashes down.
ADULT:	I wonder how we could make it stand up straighter …
JAMES:	I dunno … maybe it needs more bricks
ADULT:	That's a good idea … let's see what kind of bricks there are …
JAMES:	There are these red ones – they might fit …
ADULT:	Yes. The big square ones might make it more steady.
JAMES:	Yeah – yeah – I've found some red ones … no … they won't go.
ADULT:	Maybe we need to lie the tower on its side and take the bottom layer of bricks off first.
JAMES:	Yeah – I'll do that … can you hold that end [*tips the tower over on its side*] – look. Look … loads of bricks have come off.
ADULT:	Yes – we will have to fit these back together before we put the square red ones on.
JAMES:	Yeah … we'll do that first. Then the square ones.

In this conversation the adult and child are working through a shared problem and each of them contributes to working out the solution. The adult is playing alongside the child and has avoided using questions to allow the child to take the lead. Finally, the adult has also tried to introduce new vocabulary into the conversation along the way, such as 'square', 'straighter', 'side', 'bottom' and 'layer'. Both adult and child have several turns in the conversation, which helps the child to develop his thinking. How often do you think such extended conversations take place in your setting?

Story time

Whole group storytelling

One possibility for increasing opportunities for communication for all children during a storytelling session is to develop whole group storytelling: that is, encourage all children to say the words in the story. This approach is especially suitable for younger children and obviously the story itself must be simple and repetitive enough to lend itself to such telling, for example '*Oh Dear, No Eggs Here*' by Rod Campbell or '*We're Going on a Bear Hunt*' by Michael Rosen and Helen Oxenbury. These stories are sufficiently rhythmical to carry children along and all children have the opportunity of saying and learning the words. The role of support staff becomes much more proactive in such a scenario, as they lead the children's whole group telling of the story. This approach may be especially useful where a number of children in your group are experiencing language delay, as they gain non-pressurising experience of using whole phrases within an enjoyable whole group context.

Another way of increasing the opportunities for children to talk during storytelling sessions is to have more than one group. You could consider splitting the children into as many groups as there are staff so that best use is being made of staff time. Instead of being in a group of 20, children could then be in groups of six or seven and are likely to be able to have many more chances for active participation.

Working in small groups

Let's turn now to looking at communication opportunities and small group work in general. For staffing ratio reasons, you will be well aware that adults in early years settings cannot spend long periods of time working with children on an individual basis: you have to work with small groups to ensure that as many children as possible can work with adults during sessions. We talked above about how you can help individual children to start conversations. Here we want to look at how you can do this when working with a group of young children. Enabling children to begin conversations within a small group context is a very complex task, requiring you as adults to use a range of adult skills. Below we discuss some strategies you might find helpful in this area.

Size of the group

The size of the group is an important factor in determining how much opportunity individual children will have to talk. Clearly the younger the children the smaller the group should be. To provide good opportunities for communication within a group setting, there should be no more than four or five children in the group, fewer for 3-year-olds.

Group dynamics

The composition of the group can also play an important part in influencing the number and quality of opportunities that each child will have to speak. Where very verbal and confident children are in a group with much less confident children, it will be more difficult to ensure that all children have equal opportunities for talking and so the personalities of children will need to be taken into account. You need to consider who are the least confident talkers in your settings and perhaps be more aware of the need to group them with other such children. This may well have the result of giving these children more chance to take a more active part in the group.

Adult talk in groups

Another issue to consider when working with groups is that you need to use the same sorts of prompts as when working with individual children: that is, to use long pauses, to comment rather than question, to take part alongside children and extend what children say by adding new words. When working in a group, there are also some additional issues to be aware of. You will need to consider where children are seated in relation to you. If less confident talkers are seated opposite you, it will be easier for you to look directly across at them and encourage communication. It is also vital to look around the group continually and try to bring each child into the conversation by commenting on what each is doing by name during the course of the session.

A whole team approach

To maximise the possibility of creating an early years setting where there are many high quality opportunities for children to talk, it is vital that your whole staff team is aware of the issues and approaches discussed above. If only one or two members of staff change their practice then the benefits for children will be greatly reduced.

Those of you who manage early years settings might think of developing training sessions or at least opportunities for discussion of good practice ways of encouraging children to talk. If at all possible, these sessions should take place within normal working hours so that as many of your staff as possible can take part.

In an ideal world, there should be a number of such sessions and they should be linked to what happens in the workplace so that you and your staff can make the connection between theory and practice. Your setting might also consider developing a way of monitoring the nature of the language environment over time. If you, as a staff team, reduce your use of closed questions initially, do you continue to do so in the medium and long term?

In addition, you will need to give all new staff training on good practice ways of encouraging children to talk so that there is consistency in practice over time and despite changes to your team.

Willingness to reflect

Another key issue here is to be aware that to achieve change in any area of practice, you, as staff, need to be willing to reflect and act on the kinds of issues and approaches discussed above in relation to your own practice. This may be a challenging task because, understandably, it may often be uncomfortable to question how you have been working with children over a number of years. It may be especially difficult to change how you speak with young children.

Implications for practice

When considering new approaches, you will need to proceed cautiously and with sensitivity. In particular, there may be a need for your team to agree on some ground rules, if you decide to view video clips of your own practice, for example. You may decide, as a group, to emphasise only the positive in what you see and allowing only the staff member concerned to discuss how improvements could be made, with support from a skilled facilitator, such as a speech and language therapist known to the team. The other vital members of the team, of course, are parents and we shall explore ways of working successfully with mothers and fathers below.

Working with parents

As we know, children's primary context for learning language is the home and therefore it is essential that everyone working with young children liaises closely with mothers and fathers with regard to the development of their children's communication. A very important part of this will be valuing the very extensive knowledge that parents have of their children's development.

Practice ideas

You, as staff working in early years, will be well aware that a variety of approaches will be needed to engage parents because mothers and fathers will have very different experiences and lifestyles: one approach will not fit all. Some parents may have language and literacy difficulties and this will need to be taken account of in sensitive ways.

A range of formal and informal approaches will be necessary to work successfully with mothers and fathers. You will need to be aware that different strategies may well be necessary to ensure that fathers are successfully engaged. This may mean that you need to take account of when fathers are available and make sure that they are explicitly included in any communications and invitations. You may find it very useful to develop some father-male carer-only sessions since these have been shown to be very successful in engaging men. One of the main reasons why men often do not attend family-orientated meetings or sessions is their perception that these are for women, and indeed often there are many more women, than men in early years meetings or settings.

Of course, you will be aware of how important it is that parents should know how you are trying to develop their children's language. This may happen informally as you chat with mothers and fathers on a daily basis or it may occur within more formal situations, such as in parent support classes for those who are keen to take part. It may be helpful to develop a parent-friendly policy-type document, which describes approaches being used to get children talking in straightforward terms.

For children experiencing any delay or difficulty with their language development it will, of course, be especially important for you to make mothers and fathers aware of the approaches you are using to promote communication. You need to try to develop strategies to ensure that both parents receive this information. It may be a simple matter of addressing information specifically to mothers and fathers, both those who are living with their children and those who are not, where there are contact details.

An advanced and in-depth approach to working with parents has been developed by staff at Penn Green Children's Centre in Northamptonshire where parents of children under 3 are fully involved in the assessment and education of their young children. Parents taking part in the 'Growing Together' programme are given training in making observations of their children. The observations which parents make of their children's communication, social skills and play form the starting point for the programme. As time goes on, staff discuss children's development with parents in weekly centre-based sessions, thus placing parental knowledge at the very centre of the on-going education of their young children. Professionals running these and other groups at Penn Green have many years' experience of working with parents in these very complex ways. It is possible to visit the centre and see these approaches being put into practice at first hand.

Questions for reflection and discussion

- How many opportunities for talking with an adult do children in your setting have during a session?
- How often do children start conversations with adults in your setting?
- What kind of prompts do staff use to prompt children to talk?
- To what extent are staff using a consistent approach to developing children's communication?

 Key points for practice

- It is vital that staff adopt a whole team approach to promoting children's talk.
- You need to become aware of how you usually encourage children to talk.
- Open questions are better than closed ones. Too much use of closed questions can be unhelpful.
- It's very important that young children get a lot of experience of starting conversations.
- One of the most effective ways of encouraging young children to talk is to use long pauses, which give them time to think and speak.
- Children do most of their talking at home and therefore you need to develop ways of working closely with mothers and fathers on language development.

 Further Reading

Chivers, D. (2006) *Young Children Talking – The Art of Conversation and Why Children Need to Chatter.* London: The British Association for Early Childhood Education.

Hall, N. and Martello, J. (eds) (1996) *Listening to Children Think: Exploring Talk in the Early Years.* London: Hodder and Stoughton.

Potter, C. A. and Hodgson, S. (2007) Language enriched preschool settings: a Sure Start training approach. In J. Schneider, M. Avis and P. Leighton, (eds) *Supporting Children and Families: Lessons from Sure Start for Evidence-based Practice.* London: Jessica Kingsley.

 Useful websites

http://www.ioe.ac.uk/schools/ecpe/eppe/
http://www.ican.org.uk/
www.ican.org.uk/TalkingPoint/Frontpage.aspx
DVD: Learning to Talk, Talking to Learn: a free resource available at: www.ican.org.uk/ Make%20Chatter%20Matter/Learning%20to%20Talk.aspx
www.literacytrust.org.uk/talktoyourbaby/Initiativesnational_communicating.html
http://www.pengreen.org/index.php?unit_name=Welcome&mi_id=8

5

Stories, Storytelling and Books

Learning objectives

This chapter offers practical examples for encouraging and promoting listening to and reading stories and books from an early age. It provides ideas for using illustrations and pictures and so explores their important role in transmitting meaning and messages to readers. We will look at how to select and use stories, books and illustrations to provide quality experiences. There is a wealth of ideas on how to tell and read stories; how to develop and use varied resources for storying. The chapter looks at:

- What's so important about reading and telling stories?
- How can you capitalise on the storytelling and story reading experiences?
- Which stories and books are valuable and why?

What's so important about stories?

We have always known that reading stories to children was a worthwhile activity, but this chapter will show how much more there is to be gained from story. We can all make up stories and make our lives meaningful and interesting through the telling of stories, the relating of events. Stories in the mind (storying) are one of the most fundamental means of making meaning. Adults enjoy listening to stories on the radio, hearing stories told by friends, reading books and newspapers, as well as watching soap operas and documentaries on television. Stories are a means of learning about life, emotion, culture and morals. History, culture and family experiences have been handed down the generations through traditions of storytelling. New ideas and knowledge, history, real life issues and different characters can be explored and experienced through story. Hearing and reading stories from different genres is important, so consider the potential in traditional fairy and folk tales, myths and legends, fantasy and adventure, fiction and non-fiction, family and animal stories. In this way a rich diet of life patterns – real and imaginative – helps develop knowledge, thinking and empathy. Experience of stories therefore helps everyone to understand the world in which we live, enabling us to make connections between what we are learning and what we already know. The Early Years Foundation Stage states that you must offer opportunities for poetry, stories and non-fiction books, and this chapter should provide you with ideas about the range and rationale for these opportunities.

Stories are magic – they can take us into other worlds, times, cultures and experiences. They can mesmerise us, keeping us absorbed and intent, giving access to experiences that may be denied in real life. They offer pleasure and enjoyment in magical events and enable the development of fantasy and imagination. In a story it is possible to do anything, be anyone or anything; the possibilities are boundless, limited only by our imagination. Experience of story enriches children's imaginative play and aids understanding of character. Emotions can be safely explored and experiences of horror, tragedy and violence can be appreciated at a distance. Children can 'project' themselves into feeling and empathising non-real situations.

Listening: 'If you're sitting comfortably, then I'll begin'

You will know this phrase if you are over 50 years old. During the 1950s millions of children would sit in front of a large radio at 1.45pm and listen to a story that would follow these words. Listening to stories is an enjoyable experience. Most adults and children are drawn into the listening process, whether it is one-to-one with an adult at home or in a group in a nursery, classroom, library, theatre, museum or castle, or on television or video. Children like to hear favourite stories over and over again, enjoying the unchanging themes and familiar endings. They pay attention to rhythm and repetition, characters and events, words and meanings. There is so much to discover in a good story. From the stories they have listened to children will develop their abilities as readers, writers, storytellers and meaning makers.

Understanding language

Story is crucial for getting children to understand the structure and vocabulary of language. Stories have a pattern and structure: beginnings, middles and endings; plots and events; characters and objectives. Listening encourages anticipation, prediction, sequencing, memory, empathy, imagination and recall. It is good to introduce short repetitive stories at an early age to let children experience rhythm and cadence of language. Even if they do not acquire all the meaning of a story, children will enjoy illustrations about familiar objects and events, as well as the expression of the language. Children are able to learn how language is used and developed and you can introduce new vocabulary and grammatical structures.

In Chapter 1 we mentioned the language acquisition device for spoken language which babies are born with. We are not born with a similar device for learning to read and as we are not pre-programmed to read but have to learn how to do it, storytelling and listening to story reading are two of the most powerful routes. The enjoyment of books and their pictures can begin at a very early age for young babies, as discussed in Chapter 2. We can become totally involved in the power of story and the love of books through both listening and reading. They engage our interest, stir our emotions, develop our opinions and promote our empathy.

Literacy skills are vital in society today, and an early introduction to literacy through storytelling and using the library can provide a foundation and confidence in the use of words and communication. There are many routes into reading, and as practitioners we need to capitalise on all of them.

Why picture books and illustrations are important

Picture books and illustrations encourage children's vocabulary development, as the adult supplies the word or words for pictures. Young children soon become accomplished at matching the words with the pictures. In early stages of language acquisition they will make appropriate sounds, which gradually turn into words over time. Parents soon begin to know whether the sound being uttered is the correct 'word' for each picture, as they will have developed knowledge about their child. Animal pictures are normally a very successful way into early sound and word formation, with cows mooing, lions roaring and dogs barking. The sounds of motors, whistles, fire engines, explosions, emotions, and musical instruments are other examples. In this way children gain knowledge and experience of onomatopoeia. Children can communicate meanings through sounds before they can articulate words. They also gain familiarity of objects and concepts, which develops both their vocabulary and their knowledge and understanding of the world.

> At 6 months Amy loved this book about animals. We used to just sit together and go through it again and again. She would try to make a lot of the noises. She points to the pictures and I supply the words. I talk about the pictures, focusing on names, colours, numbers and shapes. She gets a story every night at bedtime and others during the day. There is a pile of books here that my friend gave me. We love turning pages, and turning back to the first page, don't we?

Illustrations provide images of the characters in a story, what they look like, what they are doing, what they are feeling and the setting of the story and their place in it. Margaret Meek (1991) talked about children being 'imaginative looking', as they become active and creative in discovering depths and meanings, gaining cues into the meanings being transmitted. Large picture and storybooks enable children to get physically involved in pointing out what is happening and labelling the characters and objects. Every new baby in our family is presented with a copy of the Ahlbergs' *The Baby's Catalogue*. The pictures reflect what we do in our family.

Once Upon a Time by John Prater is an excellent book that develops children's intertextuality – how the text interacts with the pictures and how to develop children's understanding of hidden meanings. In this book the main character, a young boy, tells his story of his day at home, failing to notice that famous characters from fairy tales and stories are having adventures around him. The book builds upon children's existing knowledge of these characters and they are encouraged to participate in the reading, to spot what is happening and to try to get the little boy to also notice who is there and what is happening. The witch – who could be from *The Wizard of Oz*, *Meg and Mog*, *The Worst Witch* or Hansel and Gretel's witch to name but a few – has great difficulty in navigating and steering her broomstick.

Mummy Bear is the one who actually mends Baby Bear's chair and gets Daddy Bear out of a sticky situation. One of three little pigs is really responsible for stealing Humpty Dumpty's ladder and this is why he fell off the wall! Red Riding Hood deals with the wolf – very effectively – she is having nothing to do with his invitation. One sunny Sunday afternoon, Holly, aged 2, was walking up and down the garden path stamping her foot. She was in role as Red Riding Hood dispatching her wolf in the same way – by stamping on his foot! This 2-year-old enjoyed and got a lot out of the book, but it is also really successful with primary age children to draw on all their early experiences of fairytale characters, the cause and effects of actions and events in the book. Knowledge of traditional fairy and folk tales really does play a part in young children's lives.

The following 3-year-old girls were often in role from their favourite picture books: Carmen was a wicked stepmother chanting 'Mirror mirror on the wall', allocating her parents a role in her Snow White story; Katie when wearing a shawl would say 'I'm the poor, poor peasant woman' or 'I'm Red Riding Hood' and the 'Tiger came to tea' often at Karolina's house.

 ## Bruno, age 4 years

Bruno's grandma was certain that he needed plenty of time to play through role-play and making up stories before he started to engage in formal literacy activities. Together, they derived a repertoire of simple stories based on common themes related to real life situations, using Bruno's toys as the characters in the stories, for example, getting lost, getting hurt, getting across a river. Bruno's comments of 'Will you help me?', 'Get on my back and I'll carry you' are reminiscent of the story of the Gingerbread Man. He was obviously drawing on stories he had heard and seems to have well-developed thinking skills. Bruno's grandmother believes that this natural storytelling and acting out imaginative storylines is so important.

Bruno is gaining lots of storytelling skills, which are important for future writing at school and for developing imagination. They are important for making meaning, organising thoughts cohesively, addressing an audience, sequencing events, which are all important elements of communicating with others.

What's so important about storytelling?

Children need a breadth of story experiences, a rich repertoire that requires them to listen in varied ways and so a proportion of this chapter is devoted to storytelling. This is not only to emphasise the importance of reading stories to children, but also to inspire practitioners to become confident enough to tell stories and involve children in the storytelling. Storytelling is a powerful context for the development of the spoken word. Both storytelling and story reading are important for:

- Developing language
- Promoting vocabulary through rich description; providing exciting characters and events
- Organising thought processes
- Offering complex narrative sequences
- Providing varied sentence structures
- Enjoying language for its own sake
- Most importantly, enjoying the story itself

Telling stories also shows children how they too can be storytellers and learn to create imaginative and factual happenings. This can empower children to make things happen in storytelling, and in this way confidence is developed. Children then begin to journey down the road of creativity and develop creative, imaginative thinking.

As a storyteller you can:

- Make use of voice, rhythm, tenor and songs to create pace, surprise, suspense and anticipation
- Contextualise through use of props and story resources
- Characterise through intonation, emphasis, accent, dialect
- Use gestures and movement to create effects of size, space, weather
- Create effects of mood, atmosphere and anticipation
- Create fluency and flow that suits the story
- Assess the children's listening abilities and engagement in the story
- Tell and retell favourite parts or aspects that need reiterating for effect or comprehension
- Include the children in telling and acting out the story
- Include children's names so they feel they are part of the story (this can also be a means of re-engaging a child's attention and involvement)
- Include personal and shared information to further develop a story

Reading stories to children can fire their imaginations for storytelling. By providing prompts, scaffolding and asking key questions, adults and older children can assist in developing children's vocabulary and concepts. By posing problems and challenges you can encourage children to use their imagination and enhance their storytelling skills.

Children as storytellers

You can involve children in interactive story-making by using story and nursery rhymes in circle time, explaining we can be different people. Remember that story listening and storytelling opportunities will form the basis of later literacy skills, so offer children lots of experiences, as some might not get them at home.

- Tape the stories children tell you
- Keep them for the children to listen to again and again
- Get children to develop and make meaning through their stories, through building, role-playing, painting and drawing
- Encourage children to do their own mark-making and emergent writing about the stories at a later time

Here is one such scenario from Dorota, a foundation stage teacher:

> We were doing a topic on light and dark so we built a cave of seven feet square. We aimed to develop from home, from what they know, from real experiences to imaginative. The children were involved in creating it. The cave was blacked-out inside, with different coloured reflective, fluorescent and iridescent lights going off and on intermittently. The children could change the sequences by using the control box of six different settings. There were different coloured torches, shiny CDs, holographic paper and shining stars hanging from the 'ceiling'. An adult gets in the cave with the children to tell stories relating to light and dark and modelling storytelling. The children not only wanted to be in it and found it exciting, it inspired their own stories, which became more and more imaginative. We tape what children say inside the cave and play it back to them as part of storytelling. A favourite magical story was about a bear that cannot capture the moon, which he wants to give to his mum as a present.

Story brings to life the power of imagination. Whether exploring old stories or creating new ones look for the patterns, themes, moods and pathways that build up the plot. Figure 5.1 offers some themes, to explore adapted from Mellon (1992).

Characters	Movement and pathways	Landscapes	Objects	Power
Brothers	Circling	Mountains	Keys	Darkness
Sisters	Returning	Dark towers	Treasure	Light
Wizards	Exploring	Seas and oceans	Magic swords	Love
Fairies	Searching	Doors	Crowns	Lost
Elves	Chasing	Caves	Rags	Envy
Giants	Bewitching	Castles	Gold	Greed
Cooks	Destroying	Enchanted forest	Wands	Hope
Horses	Writing	Paths	Spells	Bewilderment
Dragons	Saving	Mazes	Bread	Loyalty
Unicorns	Flying	Winter	Magic lamp	Bravery

Figure 5.1 Themes for storytelling

Family and heritage stories

A recurrent theme in this book is the two-way process of involving parents and families and capitalising on what they can offer. Family stories and heritage stories are important as they create a shared history and a bond. They can be more interesting than fictional stories for children, who love real stories. They tell of a previous time when parents and grandparents were younger and actually had 'real adventures'. These are real stories about real people. Sharing stories from the past can be particularly important for children whose parents were brought up in a different country. Oral culture and sharing stories can awaken a child's curiosity and help them to gain an interest in their own unique heritage and culture. Children and adults alike enjoy the facts in the stories and that these family fables are so similar to stories they read in books. Young children will often ask for family stories to be repeated again and again. The following was a favourite with Sadie.

Jonathan's Story – 1954

When I was about 8 years old, the circus came to town. The message went round that the elephants were coming by train and tension grew. From the school playing field, you could just about see the railway station, where a big crowd was gathering. All the children who'd gone home for dinner hadn't come back for school. Others were getting so excited they jumped over the railings and didn't come back. Eventually, I jumped over the railings. At the station there were lots of children, policemen and circus people; the fire engine and ambulance were also there. You could hear elephants in the carriages, getting excited. As the elephants shouted, the children pushed closer. There was an announcement – if we didn't move back, the elephants wouldn't come out. Eventually, the children moved back and five elephants were allowed out of the carriages. Two or three of them trumpeted loudly. We followed the elephants down the middle of the road. When we got to the main road, the policeman held up his hand, but the elephants didn't stop and the children kept running, shouting and cheering. All the traffic had to be stopped. All the people in the market place stopped work and watched us. One of the boys in our class, Dennis, was very brave and kept going up and patting the elephants. We followed them to the circus tent and the elephants went inside and were given lots of straw to eat. Everybody then had to turn back. I was lost, but fortunately, I met other boys from school, who knew the way back.

When told in the first person, a story can become more exciting, real and part of life. Children find it hard to envisage a time when they were not around. Through these oral storytellings of events in a family's past, children can visualise characters, places and occurrences for themselves. The links between facts and fiction can be developed through children's imagination. Stories can be embellished further and extra anecdotes inserted. Through family stories children can gain knowledge about sequences of events and about cause and effect.

The following story relates the humble beginnings of a local doctor, whose children would probably never have recalled this incident, had it not been relayed to them over and over as they were growing up in England.

Sama's Story – 1954

When Sama was a young doctor, his first appointment was in a remote Indian village, very rural and far from Hydrabad. He took his wife, Bala, and their two young boys, aged 3 years and 18 months. They packed all their possessions that could be carried and travelled by bus for nearly a whole day to get to the village. They arrived close to the village at about 7 o'clock in the evening, but between the road and the village was a river. It had been the rainy season and the bus couldn't cross the river. Sama, Bala and the children were put off the bus and Sama had to wade across the river carrying the family's possessions. He returned for his wife, then each of the children. He had to make many crossings. When they all got to the other side of the river the people in the village took them to their house and surgery and left them alone. They were all wet and tired from the journey. Bala put the children to bed and then she cried. She did not know what they had come to; she wanted to go home. The following morning they were awakened by all the villagers bringing gifts and food. They were all delighted to have a doctor in the village. Sama and his family stayed there for five years. He performed many operations and looked after the health of everyone in the village. It was a very happy time in their lives.

What is most important in these two stories from Jonathan and Sama, however, is the richness of the cultural heritage and family history. Stories such as these really support and develop children's sense of self-identity – where they come from and how they relate to others' identity and experiences – knowledge of self and knowledge of others. This is particularly important in the culturally rich United Kingdom today, where children from many diverse backgrounds live side by side in community. Young children love to hear, retell and talk about their own and their family stories: what they did as babies, a visit to Grandma's and when Uncle Lewis came to stay. These can be linked to photographs and birthday cards enabling children to talk about time, about yesterday and 'when I was a baby'. Stories created around personal history therefore have social and emotional value for real life experiences and true situations. Children need to tell stories about what happened at the shops, nursery and in the playground to both parents and practitioners. From a young age they can tell anecdotes and reminisce, so encourage this type of story-telling in your setting. These personal stories are important in helping children make sense of their world.

Invite families to contribute by coming in to tell their stories, sharing them in writing, tape recording them or creating a booklet of stories. There is so much value in family stories that can be passed down the generations. Also encourage parents to contribute to profiles and record books about their children. Don't forget to tell your own stories to children – even 3-year-olds will be interested in what you do out of the setting – they probably think you live in a cupboard at night waiting for them to return to you the next day!

Turning the pages together

We're Going on a Bear Hunt

This mum of three boys aged 2, 3 and 10, talks about the importance of books and stories in their lives. She thinks it is quite unusual for boys to be so book-orientated, but she is a keen reader and has modelled reading to them, which has cultivated their love of books.

> Our evening routine involves all of us in story-time before bed. We have masses of books at home and the boys pick the one they want to read. However, the other week Owen brought 'The Bear Hunt' from pre-school library, but he wouldn't take it back so I had to buy it. Every night, when asked which story they wanted, the boys answered 'The Bear Hunt'. As I read it the two youngest boys act it out. They love the squelch, squelch, squelch part, and hide under the duvet at the end when the bear is coming after them. Even though they are just 2 and 3 they know the lines at the end where it says, 'We're not scared', and they anticipate and shout it out before I have a chance to read it aloud.

The Little Mouse, the Red Ripe Strawberry and the Big Hungry Bear

Four boys aged between 3 and 6 helped make a landscape of mountains, moorland, forest, rocks, river and fields with papier mâché, gardening materials, pebbles, shells, sand and gravel. The landscape was to create an environment to promote imaginative play and storytelling. The following is one of the stories created and told by 3-year-old Tim using the playscape he helped make. It is evident that his story has been inspired from listening to his father reading *The Little Mouse, the Red Ripe Strawberry and the Big Hungry Bear*. His older brother, Jonas, aged 6, has also played an important part in Tim's developing his accomplished storytelling, acting as a role model through telling his story first.

TIM:	One day was a mouse who said I'm going to go out hunting. So we went back inside and got his big ladder. He climbed over the rock.
DAD:	What did he need the big ladder for?
TIM:	To get the big, ripe strawberry.
DAD:	Oh. Where's the big, ripe strawberry?
TIM:	It's here. It went over his house, all over. Then he was right by the big, ripe strawberry. So he climbed. So he put his ladder up and tied a knot on it.
DAD:	But Mr. Mouse, have you heard about…?
TIM:	The big hungry bear? So he gets the top down and he went aaarrrhhh but he didn't get the big, ripe strawberry. So he had another go. Then he got it and he picked it off with his nose. Weee!
DAD:	He picked it off with his nose?
TIM:	Yes. That one's for you.
DAD:	What are we doing now? Are we sharing it? Why?
TIM:	Because everyone wants one.
DAD:	Not because the big hungry bear will get it?
TIM:	That one's for you. That one's for you.
IRENI:	Thank you. I love strawberries.
TIM:	And that one's for me.
IRENI:	Mmmm.
JONAS:	It's making me hungry this.
TIM:	Oh, the big hungry bear's here so I better get mine quickly. I ate all of mine in one go, that's why I'm all fat. And he puts his big ladder back. There. He didn't think where he could go now because he was listening to the wind.
JONAS:	I'll do the wind.
IRENI:	That's a good sound.
DAD:	Is that the end Tim?
TIM:	No. But I am stopping doing it because Jonas is doing something.
IRENI:	He's making the wind blow. I wonder if mouse will get blown away.
JONAS:	Aarrrhhh!
IRENI:	He's getting blown away. Oh no! He needs to be low, doesn't he, so the wind can't take him away. If he goes up high, he'll get blown away by the wind.
JONAS:	Brrrrrr! Wooooo!
TIM:	That's the end because he got killed.

The purpose of the landscape is to get children to tell their own stories. If they have had experiences of stories being told and read they will naturally do storying in their play. As Tim does in the above scenario, they will develop their own characters, dialogue and actions. Whitehead (2004) states that being able to place ourselves right in the centre of a story is a valuable start to becoming a reader and writer. Listen to children when they are playing and see if you can determine the storying elements and which stories they are using in their play.

Storytelling using a playscape 'Where's the big hungry bear?'

Where the Wild Things Are

Where the Wild Things Are by Maurice Sendak has been a long-term favourite of children, parents and educators. It is not a long story, but the sentences can be drawn out to gain full effect, and the potential for audience participation is great. There is so much ono-matopoeia in this story – the gnashing of teeth, growling voice and the stressing of the 'r' in rolling, all add to the sound effects. The message of the story is also important – no matter how badly Max behaves or what he does, his home and his supper will always be there! However, it is the way that language is used that is so wonderful and children request the story again and again. It is now possible to buy puppets of Max and the mon-sters with which children can tell their own stories. *Where the Wild Things Are* offers rich opportunities for drama. Children can create monster masks from card or papier mâché moulded on a balloon then cut in half, elasticated for facemasks or attached to canes to hand-hold. The masks allow the children to become monsters and act out the physical expressions and sound effects. You can add a long piece of blue material for the sea; create a boat from large building blocks or large wooden box and use 'In Hall of the Mountain King', music from Greig's *Peer Gynt suite No. 1, Opus 46*, so the children can engage in Max's wild rumpus!

Story and role-play

Story can enrich all areas of the curriculum, acting as a springboard into an area or topic of learning. It can be a starting point or vehicle to carry knowledge or particular skills. Story is a useful medium with which to stimulate a play situation where role-play can be planned and developed effectively. It is a vehicle for transporting both ideas and imagination. Role-play can involve using real life articles, materials or furniture to represent the physical environment.

> When teaching in an inner city school, I found a carpet in the caretaker's house. I told the children it was magic. It took us on journeys to enchanted places, it helped us to think and get on with work. The children always behaved on the carpet; they respected, listened and discussed with each other, as well as telling stories.

Socio-dramatic experiences enable children to participate in unthreatening role-play situations where the targeted language can be promoted without a fear of failure or production to an audience. Figure 5.2 gives some examples of stories that can be used to stimulate role-play.

Theme	Story	Author
Car/garage	*Mr Gumpy's Journey*	John Burningham
Builder's yard	*The House that Jack Built*	Traditional
Farm	*Fantastic Mr Fox*	Roald Dahl
Fire station	*The Fire Across the Street*	Manju Gregory
Forest	*Hansel and Gretel*	Traditional
Museum	*Lulu and the Flying Babies*	Posy Simmonds
Pet shop	*Mitthu the Parrot*	Susheila Stone
Post Office	*The Jolly Postman*	Allan Ahlberg
Seashore	*Bimwili and Zimwi*	Verna Aardema
Washday/laundry	*Mrs Mopple's Washing Line*	Anita Hewett
Weather station	*Bringing the Rain to Kapiti Plain*	Verna Aardema

Figure 5.2 Stories and role-play

Involving artists

The following scenarios describe how artists – dramatists, storytellers, puppeteers – visit settings to get children involved in stories and storytelling.

World Book Day

World Book Day was designated by UNESCO as a worldwide celebration of books and reading in over 100 countries. World Book Day became an event at one inner city school, where everyone was involved in storytelling, story reading and dressing up as characters from books. As well as being great fun, the opportunities for talk and storytelling were numerous. Maggie Power, storyteller and lecturer, describes the day's events:

 World Book Day at an inner city school

Everyone arrived in different costumes, clutching their favourite storybook. The adults arrived dressed as Red Riding Hood, Little Miss Muffett, Snow White and others. Among the children were Harry Potter, Superman, a dinosaur hunter, a creature from outer space, fairies and princes that glittered and glowed from various swords, wands and jewels. Red Riding Hood took the school assembly and the children literally pulsed with excitement as they looked around. A group from each class came forward, explaining their costume and its link to their favourite book. Some costumes were simple – a pair of Spiderman pyjamas with some embellishments – others wore shoes, tiaras, hats or held plastic swords and shields.

One father, a puppeteer, had everyone listening to his stories. I shared one of my favourite African stories about an ostrich that wanted to fly like his friends. Two of the children acted the parts of the two main birds – the ostrich and the sparrow. I provided the words for them to interact and speak to each other. All the 5-year-olds became an 'oral' orchestra, providing the sound track that accompanied the telling, making the sound of the warm breeze as it fluttered in the trees, the bangs and crashes of the ostrich as he failed at all of his attempts at flying. At the very end they were able to share the joy of the ostrich, as he found himself flying through the air, but then his annoyance at finding there were none of his friends around to share his excitement. The ostrich's friends were making it possible for him to fly by holding him in the air with vines and creepers attached to his flying machine. It was a complicated story for such young children, but they were involved and entranced. It is a testimony to the power of story that it can captivate and engage even the very young, maintaining their concentration all morning.

You can do this too in your setting:

- Ensure your stories reflect a child's home and cultural knowledge, enabling them to build on what they clearly know
- Don't limit children's story and imaginative experiences
- Provide children with words and chunks of language to use in stories
- Model new structures or chunks of language repetitively through story
- Puppets are valuable to tell stories to children, and for children to use to tell stories
- Story tapes enable children to listen again and again, internalising phrases and chunks of language

Storybox Project

The Storybox Project in the 1990s involved artists such as puppeteers, video-makers, poets, storytellers, theatre groups, dramatists and lantern-makers visiting schools. These artists not only 'performed' for the children they engaged the children in performance and creation of dramatic props. They modelled a 'creation' or 'installation' and then the children would work individually in pairs, in groups and in classes to create something of their own. Lois Lambert was a shadow puppeteer, who normally performed her shows in rural settings, in total darkness, in the Far East. The performance had few words; its messages and stories came through visual images and movements of the shadow puppets and the music. She created a show of light and dark, her large homemade puppet theatre was probably 10 feet tall and lit by flames! Can you imagine that she recreated her torch-lit performance in a school hall? The audience was spellbound. Her shadow puppets were intricately created from the cut-out images. These were attached to long canes and the children were taught how to hold up the shadow puppets and move them toward and away from the theatre 'screen'. The children then made their own shadow puppets, wrote their own plays and performed them for each other in English, Gujerati and Punjabi. Lois was certainly an inspiration for the school.

Suitcase full of stories

A suitcase full of precious objects that are highly tactile and visual, prompting rich descriptions can interest and excite young children's storytelling. Sarah Argents worked in three nurseries in Wales with her early years project 'a suitcase full of stories', which was funded by the Core Duffield Foundation through its Small Grants Programme for Performing Arts Education. Sarah chose objects which she 'anticipated would arouse children's curiosity and provide a stimulus for the creation of stories'. 'The opening of a suitcase – lined with purple and gold silk – regularly resulted in gasps of delight and wonder at the beautiful objects within.' Sarah had been inspired by Vivian Gussin Paley's storytelling work in a nursery in Chicago, where children were encouraged to construct stories through careful questioning. The stories were then written down exactly as told. Her second inspiration was through a project in which Italian nursery nurses worked with a theatre company in Bologna creating a performance 'Una valigia ... tante storie' – 'One suitcase ... many stories'. Initially Sarah prompted the children with – How would you like to tell your story? Once upon a time ... There was once a ...? What did the bee do next? Whose ironing board is it? – but they soon began to launch into their stories without assistance. Example of the children's stories and photographs of the precious objects can be viewed on-line at www.theatriolo.com/news/suitcase.htm

Story and foreign language learning

Story is an excellent way to teach a modern foreign language (MFL) to children. Through a familiar or traditional story, children can learn key words in another language. For example, *Goldilocks and the Three Bears* was adapted by Sheila Hébert Collins in 'Jolie Blonde and the Three Héberts', and incorporates two languages as illustrated in this excerpt overleaf:

'Jolie Blonde sat down and took a big bite from the big bowl. "C'est chaud!" she said. Then she took a bite from the medium bowl and said "Mais non! C'est froid!" Finally, she took a bite from the little bowl and said, "Ummm ... ça c'est bon!" And she ate it all up!
C'est chaud! (say sho) – that's hot!
Mais non! (meh nonh) – oh no!
C'est froid! (say fwah) – that's cold!
Ça c'est bon! (sah say bonh) – that is good!'

Children love to be able to speak in another language. The success of the television programme *Dora the Explorer* and the promotion of Spanish is one testimony to the value of promoting an MFL to young children. At some nurseries a different language is promoted every week to give children multilingual experiences and to promote language awareness.

Children at the library: selecting information books

Parents should be encouraged to take their children to their local library. If children can get used to using the library and its resources at an early age, then they will feel confident about handling books, reading stories and finding information from reference books to support later learning. Of course parents can take their children to a bookshop, but it would be impossible to purchase the extensive range of books potentially available through the library, and libraries provide reading opportunities free of charge!

Joseph demonstrates how he controls the choice of books and the dialogue with his mother, when a book about the sea and boats fascinates him. He selected a book about the *Titanic*, which was full of detailed pictures. It is a true story and though Joseph obviously cannot comprehend the real tragedy, he is learning to understand through the information the book provides. Joseph asks a myriad questions about boats, ships, oil, guns, pirates, skeletons, icebergs, floating and sinking.

MUM:	It sank
JOSEPH:	Why?
MUM:	It hit an iceberg
JOSEPH:	Did people die?
MUM:	That's like the boat we saw in Whitby
JOSEPH:	That one that came in? How did that iceberg get there?
MUM:	It was there all the time.
JOSEPH:	Where's the bit that crashed? I wish I was going on one of those boats
MUM:	Oh, you don't, lots of people died
JOSEPH:	Did they turn into skeletons?
MUM:	Perhaps they did
JOSEPH:	Does it show you lots of skeletons?
JOSEPH:	Look at that submarine

Joseph's mother comments:
'Joseph is fascinated by the non-fiction. I couldn't provide him with all this. This environment is great. He doesn't run round or shout here.'

Some books are a mixture of fact and fiction and some include stories about violence, fighting and skeletons and Joseph loves the action and adventure. If it is difficult for children in your area to visit a library then create your own. One nursery successfully got children into borrowing, reading and returning books to their self-made 'library'. A nursery nurse modelled being a librarian, then the children took on the role. It promoted a lot of shared reading, talking about pictures and story.

What is your story corner like? Think about:

- Comfort, accessibility, lighting, levels of seating
- Presentation and quality of books
- Borrowing by children and parents
- Variety of stories and books
- Pictures, illustrations, photographs
- Dual language and multicultural books
- Children-made books
- Story tapes and DVDs
- Flap-up, 3D, paper technology
- Display
- Story costumes, puppets to use in telling stories
- Collections of books
- Poetry, rhyme, song books
- Story sacks
- Practical objects that are mentioned in stories

Many of the examples in this chapter have been about boys. This was not deliberate – these examples have been provided by families and practitioners and hopefully should dispel the myth that boys are less interested in literacy than girls. The examples show that boys have a love of story and are very capable of storytelling. Where they might have more difficulty is in being directed to formal literacy experiences that they are not ready for, and this will be explored in Chapter 7. The best means of optimising language development in children is to find ways to link the written and spoken word by choosing good literature that stimulates children's imagination. In so doing, inevitably both skills of listening and speaking are simultaneously utilised and therefore acquisition is intensified. The next chapter demonstrates how rhyme, rhythm, sound and song, along with story, are also very important foundations for language and literacy development.

 Questions for reflection and discussion

- Do you communicate a love of story to children?
- Will you have a go at storytelling to and with children?
- Observe young children playing and see if you can determine where stories influence their play.
- Do the books in your setting reflect diversity – genre, heritage and format?

Key points for practice

- Listening to stories is very enjoyable; reading and telling stories to children are very worthwhile
- Everyone in a setting can be involved in storytelling
- A breadth of stories and books is important
- Early story experiences can make a huge difference to language development
- Stories and books are the routes into literacy
- Story is an excellent springboard into cross-curricular learning

 Further Reading

Grugeon, E. and Gardner, P. (2000) *The Art of Storytelling for Teachers and Pupils*. London: David Fulton.
Sharp, E. (2005) *Learning Through Talk*. London: Sage.
Toye, N. and Prendiville, F. (2000) *Drama and Traditional Story in the Early Years*. London: Routledge Falmer.

 Useful websites

www.literacytrust.org.uk
http://www.realbooks.co.uk/articles/favouritebooks.html
http://www.collaborativelearning.org/foundationonline.html
www.worldbookday.com
http://www.storyarts.org

6

Rhyme, Rhythm, Sound and Song

 Learning objectives

This chapter looks at the importance of rhyme, rhythm, sound and song for developing young children's language and literacy skills. Practitioners should offer these through playful multisensory activities that encourage enthusiasm and enjoyment. The connections between physical movement and brain development will be explored to show why it is important that young children engage in rhythm and movement. Research has shown how children's early experience of nursery rhymes and songs have a direct correlation to literacy success at school. The development of phonological awareness in children in meaningful and practical ways will be explored, along with how to promote children's playfulness with phonics and sounds. This chapter will consider:

- Why rhyme, rhythm, sound and song are important aspects of children's language development.
- How these can be utilised effectively in the classroom.
- Different perspectives on how to promote phonics.

The Early Years Foundation Stage (DfES, 2007a) requires that you promote opportunities for children to:

- Share and enjoy a wide range of rhymes, music and songs
- Link language with physical movement in action songs and rhymes
- Develop children's phonological awareness through small group and individual teaching

It is essential that young children gain knowledge of real-life sounds, songs, rhymes, and rhythm before phonic instruction begins. It takes a confident practitioner to ensure that their children gain a thorough grounding in these skills before moving on to formal teaching of sounds. This is not to decry the importance of developing phonological experiences, but it needs to be paced in appropriate time and context. You need to be able to determine children's individual needs and how early sound, song and rhythm experiences need to be developed in order that a true understanding and therefore application occurs. So let us start at the very beginning by considering the first sounds we hear.

First sounds

The first sound a child hears is the mother's heartbeat while still in the womb. For the unborn child, this rhythm signifies power and safety. Newborns continue to tune into this sound and rhythm. They hear and feel this 'music' – quickly recognising sounds, which they begin to make their own. Encourage parents and carers to capitalise on this – to talk, sing and even coo to their babies, and tune children into the sounds they will produce in their language. You should listen to how babies try out new sounds; watch, respond and join in with them. Also, listen to what they are saying; spend longer time with them so that you can tune the ear to each individual baby's attempts at communication. In so doing, you will gain a greater understanding of the sounds and pronunciation they generate and of what they need.

Rhyme, rhythm, songs and music are an important element of early language development. In an experiment conducted among pregnant women, nursery rhymes were played repeatedly and it was evident that the babies recognised these tunes immediately after birth. Other experiments revealed that infants responded to the theme tunes of soap operas watched by their mothers in the final weeks leading up to the birth (http://www.sciencemaster.com/columns/wesson/wesson_part_07.php). What is taking place is that the stimulated brain cells (neurons) transmit messages to those neurons which are specifically responsible for interpreting sound. These neurons make decisions about what sounds are important, distinguishing for example between the sound of a car horn, tyres screeching and the language of the mother, which will ultimately become the child's first language. They perform an important function in the process of language development for babies.

Communicating through making music

The heartbeat is in fact the fundamental rhythm for all of us, reverberating inside our bodies, so that we all have the capacity to become musicians. Music is communication, so musical games and playing with instruments are ways of communicating with babies and young children. Talk to Your Baby at www.talktoyourbaby.org.uk and Music One2One at www.education.ex.ac.uk/music-one2one have developed activity packs and posters to promote the benefits of music. Parents and carers are advised to provide a variety of music, sing favourite songs, clap in rhythm and explore moving and dancing to music.

You can prepare to make music by becoming aware of the nature and range of noise and sound – that sounds have beat, rhythm, timbre, tone, sequence, resonance, echo. Try the following activities with babies as well as young children.

- Create sound effects with voice, whistling, humming
- Use bodies to create sound – use hands, feet, chest, knees, head for clapping, stamping, clicking, banging
- Beat out the rhythm and syllables of each child's name
- Tap objects' and toys' names on the items themselves
- Repeat sounds and get children to appreciate the rhythm of syllables within words
- Learn language through song and music
- Make sure sound resources are in the treasure baskets – with wooden spoons and pots
- Make musical instruments – shakers containing rice, beans, seeds, marbles, buttons

Twins reading rhymes together

All these activities are very important for early language development, but also pay off in developing early literacy through developing the phonological awareness that is an important reading skill.

With older children you can use a wider range of resources to create sound and music. Consider having a music area in your setting, use instruments in circle time and play games. One idea is to have a child play a musical instrument behind a screen and others have to choose an instrument that matches the sound. Outside you can tie a washing line between posts and intersperse small and large saucepans, frying pans and copper tubing of different lengths to get a variation of notes and sounds. Children can hit them with a range of implements such as wooden and metal ladles and spoons. Children can beat out rhythms, make music, create tunes and adults can support through modelling beats, rhythms and tunes.

Communicating through song

It is not as common nowadays to hear adults singing lullabies, yet this is an important way of communicating with and soothing babies. Parents need to exploit children's enjoyment of singing; and parents don't need to be highly skilled – babies are mostly non-judgemental! And yet it is all too rare to hear parents singing to their children. Parents will have fun with their young children: through singing, exploring music and movement, and children soon cue into singing games and songs. There is strong research evidence that exposure to and knowledge of songs and rhymes promote success in early literacy development.

There is real value in parents' being involved in playgroups, as they can learn to sing the same songs with their children at home. Harvey's mum says he has always loved songs since being little, but she didn't know all the ones they sing at playgroup. She really enjoys doing her stint at playgroup because *she* learns so much. Harvey, aged nearly 3, has adapted the 'Tommy Thumb' song and now does the actions with his toys, 'Mickey mouse where are you?' If parents are unable to spend time in your setting, suggest they might buy or borrow a tape or CD that has many of the songs you are singing with the children. One setting created a song mobile that had the songs written out for parents and students to select just in case they did not know all the words.

> At 18 months old, Jessie was obviously trying to communicate something to her family, but the meaning was lost on both her grandfather and mother. She kept saying 'uhh' and touching her head, and chest, then her knees and toes. At last Jessie's face lit up when finally Grandma recognised what she was doing and began to sing to her 'Heads, shoulders, knees and toes'. Before she could even speak, this baby knew all her body parts because she was familiar with this song. She could not say the words, but on request touched her nose, head, knees etc.

This is similar to Yuki, who is of Japanese and English heritage and who was touching her nose, eyes and other parts of her body when asked to by her mother in both languages. This is also before she can even say the words. This child has done baby signing and her mother thinks it seems to have enhanced both her desire and ability to communicate. As Ava's mum commented:

> We tried the singing and sign classes last week and so we are trying to teach her. I don't think we have got very far yet, but it is quite interesting going into the class and seeing those that are at the end of it. They are so excited – singing the songs and doing the movements – seeing them actually doing it is quite amazing. They are doing 'The elephant went through the jungle' and we are learning to mime the actions.

As referred to in Chapter 2, one setting used magnetic story boards to support practice. It is fascinating to see all ages participating in the storytelling, whether they are babies, toddlers or 3–5s.

The practitioner is confident and happy singing to and with children, even in front of visiting audiences: 'Alice the camel has three humps, three humps, three humps. Alice the camel has three humps ...' The children move near to the magnetic boards for the song and some are very practised at handling the laminated characters. Everyone joins in by moving, singing and shaking the characters.

The stories, rhymes and songs follow the children's interests and their ability is taken into account. For example the songs for babies will be shorter and contain less numbers. The setting is now promoting a 'song of the week', and to involve parents more is providing them with copies of the song, which includes information about the 'familiar' tune to which it is to be sung. Staff will even sing a tune for the parents so that they become familiar with it. Favourites are:

- 'Goldilocks went to the house with the three bears'
- 'Five currant buns in a baker's shop'
- 'Hickory dickory dock'
- 'I'm a little teapot'

Young children need to be supported in their early attempts at singing songs. Many children get music and singing experiences at home and so it is easier to capitalise on this in a setting. It is not necessary to get all the words correct but to model, prompt, praise and apprentice children into learning the words of a song. Here is Marie with her family – a total of three adults – who join in with her singing.

I: How does 'Postman Pat' go?
M: Postman PAT, Postman PAT with a white cat, with the white cat. I don't know the other bit.
K: Early in the morning as the sun is dawning, Bob says he's a really happy cat.
M: Early in the morning, er as the sun is snoring ... cat.
I: Postman –
M: PAT, Postman Pat and his back n white cat CAT.
K: Postman PAT, Postman Pat and his black and white cat.
M: Early in the morning, early in the morning – don't know the other bit.
D: Pat he is a really happy man.
M: *man.*
K: Oh, I said chap! [*Laughing.*]
D: Everybody knows his bright red van.
M: Red van.

To encourage sound and song you could:

- Create a bag of animals for Old MacDonald's Farm
- Collect models of a spider, crocodile, cat, mouse and get children to select an object from the pump bag to prompt the song
- Make songs personal for children through including their names in a song

When Glen hurt himself and started to cry I sat him on my knee, wrapped him in my arms and while rocking to and fro I began to sing. I sang to the tune of a song I knew 'There's no-one quite like Glen, I know you will agree, he's very cute and cuddly and sitting on my knee.' His tears soon subsided and he and his brother were howling with laughter shouting, 'Sing it again, sing it again!'

Children will incorporate familiar songs into their play. The following scenario is of two children on a roundabout in the park adapting 'The Wheels on the Bus' into their play and singing:

> Tummy going round and round
> Tummy going round and round
> My tummy was going round and round
> My back was going round and round
> Mine was going fast
> My tummy was going round again

As children get more proficient at rhyming, they will do more of this interchanging of words. 'The Wheels on the Bus' also inspired the creation of a bus in one playgroup. The chairs were arranged and there were numbers on the chairs. The children bought tickets, counted out pennies and matched numbers to chairs. They sang on the bus, got in role as characters through wearing different hats and went on an imaginary bus ride.

Rhymes

The importance of young children listening, singing and saying rhymes has been well researched and substantiated. From research done by Goswami and Bryant (1990), and Bryant et al. (1989), we know that this early knowledge eases children into early phonemic development and can make a real difference to beginning and developing reading skills. But rhymes are also important as they support children's sentence structure and vocabulary development. Young children can learn very complicated words through acquiring them in rhymes and songs. They manage to learn: 'Mary, Mary, quite contrary'. Rhymes also contribute to children's concept of story and to their pleasure in language for its own sake.

Children enjoy traditional rhymes and so learn about sequences, events, motives, causes and effects (Cooper, 2004). Most cultures have their own long-established rhymes and they can be an important part of heritage and life experience. They are often based on everyday events and aspects of life such as washing day or the weather: 'Rain, rain go away'; 'Here we go round the mulberry bush'; 'Zła zima' (see later in this section). Some nursery rhymes are set in the past and are historical sources: 'Ring a Ring of Roses'; 'Rock a Bye Baby (a Caribbean lullaby); 'Grand Old Duke of York'.

MUM:	What shall we sing?
FRANKIE:	Grand Old Duke of York
MUM:	Can you sing all that? Go on then
FRANKIE:	Em, Grand Old Duke of York, he had ten thousand men, marched em up to the top o the ill, and marched em down again, and when they were up they were up, and when they were down they were down, and when they were only alt way up dey were up not down.
MUM:	Well done!

Rhymes occur naturally in everyday activities:

LEE:	Teddy Bear, Teddy Bear go up stair, Teddy Bear, Teddy Bear say your prayer
DAD:	Go on Lee, keep singing
LEE:	Teddy Bear, Teddy Bear go up stair
LEE and DAD [*together*]:	Teddy Bear, Teddy Bear say your prayer

MUM:	What's this Matt?
MATT:	'pider 'pider
MUM:	Yes, it's a spider. Shall we sing 'Incey, Wincey Spider'?
MATT:	Spider up spout
[Matt and his mother sing 'Incey, Wincey Spider']	

Rhymes are fun and children love to sing and chant them. In the beginning they will not be able to pronounce all the words, but will jog along with the rhythm, gradually adding more and more words. Adults continue to model the correct words and with practice children get more and more competent and articulate. Halina and Dad are singing nursery rhymes whilst Halina is on the rocking horse. She sings along, joining in the last words – the rhyming words – with exclamations and shouts.

DAD:	Horsey horsey don't you stop
HALINA:	Stop
DAD:	Down the road go clippity clop
HALINA:	Clippy clop. Horsey you stop
HALINA:	Daddy just doing it
DAD:	Does the horse have to go for you to sing it? Horsey horsey don't you stop Just let your feet go clippity clop. Swish your tail
HALINA:	Horseys eat you all up
DAD:	They can't
HALINA:	They do

One student turned a reading area in a nursery setting into a nursery rhyme village. This included Mary, Mary's cottage and garden, Humpty Dumpty's wall with soldiers, Jack and Jill's hill and well with pails of water. The children learnt and chanted the rhymes. They created their own stories through playing with the characters in the nursery rhyme environment, taking on roles and extending the rhyme scenarios. Try using a nursery rhyme in circle time to show how we can take on roles and be different people.

You need to provide children with a repertoire of varied rhymes and poems. When going up and down stairs or steep hills with children encourage counting through rhythm and rhyme: '1, 2, 3, 4, 5, Once I caught a fish alive'; 'One potato, two potato'; 'Hot cross buns'. One nursery created a pulley system to pull Incey Wincey Spider up the spout and the mouse up the clock for 'Hickory Dickory Dock'. These all involve matching words to physical actions, which is a great way to learn numbers and rhyme. Lots of rhymes promote gross motor movement and allow the children to become totally involved – think of the physical actions promoted in 'Humpty Dumpty'.

Also think about:

- Traditional rhymes
- Nursery rhymes
- Finger rhymes
- Action rhymes
- Counting rhymes
- Humorous rhymes
- Short poems
- Dual language rhymes

Bryant et al (1989) found that the number of nursery rhymes known by pre-school children predicted later reading success. Writing out familiar rhymes, laminating and hanging them from a mobile makes them accessible to adults and parents working in or visiting a setting. In this way rhyme becomes a natural event in every child's day. The staff at one children's centre created song and rhyme bags containing playful resources and laminated song cards for 'Five Little Ducks', 'Dr Foster went to Gloucester' and 'Twinkle, Twinkle' for parents and children to borrow and sing at home. These bags contained visual and malleable resources to support children's learning of the songs and rhymes and also to extend the adults' repertoire. Having a range of these can broaden children's language and singing experiences, and also their cultural experiences. Songs in different home languages not only promote children's developing bilingualism, but are also a link to their heritage. Get both parents' and children's support in the singing, rhyming and reading of their culture's stories, songs and rhymes.

Rhyming in Polish

There is a growing number of Polish children entering settings, as their parents take up the opportunity to work in the UK. These children need their language, culture and heritage valued in the same way as the children described in Chapter 3. Rhyme and song is an ideal way to capitalise on their linguistic experiences and the knowledge they bring to a setting's staff and children. 'Zła zima' (pronounced 'Zwa zhima') is a very traditional Polish rhyme – young children sing this in kindergartens in Poland. It is very good for rhythm, song and drama play. These lines are the chorus:

Hu hu ha; hu hu ha! Nasza zima zła.
Hu hu ha; hu hu ha! Nasza zima zła.
[*Translation*: Hu hu ha; hu hu ha! Our bad winter]

The children sing the song and do the actions – rubbing their noses and ears, miming a snowstorm blowing into their eyes, and moving their bodies to struggle against the wind. This is a really tuneful catchy song. You could try prompting Polish children with the first two lines and they will probably respond with the whole poem for you. Why not ask Polish parents to come into your setting and teach the children the rhyme?

The meaning of the song is that it is important to be strong, not to be afraid, to cope with a bad winter, to meet the struggle with bad weather in a positive way through laughter and play. Temperatures in Polish winters can reach as low as minus 20 degrees! Sometimes the snow can last weeks at a time and so affects all aspects of life. It is part of Polish children's education to develop a positive attitude to coping when life is difficult. So it can be seen that rhymes have multiple purposes. Polish has many sounds that are difficult for other speakers to acquire. It is very useful, however, if we can not only support children's language and culture, but also have an appreciation of how their language works and what sounds they have acquired in their first language. Let's look at an example, using 'The Enormous Turnip,' which is not only a very traditional story in England but is also a well-known Polish rhyme. Here are a couple of verses, first in English, then in Polish:

One day Granddad planted a turnip seed in the garden
It grew big and strong
He pulled and pulled
But he couldn't do it.

Zasadził dziadek rzepkę w ogrodzie,
Wyrosła rzepka jędrna I krzepka
Więc ciągnie rzepkę dziadek nieboże
Ciągnie I ciągnie, wyciągnąć nie może!

He asked Grandma to help him
'I hold the turnip, you hold me'
They pulled and pulled
But they couldn't do it.

Zawołał dziadek na pomoc babcie
'Ja złapię rzepkę, ty za mnie złap się!'
I biedny dziadek z babcią niebogą
Ciągną I ciągną, wyciągnąć nie mogą!

Could you read the Polish version? It is not easy – there are many new sounds and phonemic representations. Below is a phonetic transcription.* See if you can manage it. Test it out on young Polish children and get them to show their language awareness. They will be delighted to correct you!

Zasaju jardek zhebkown ve ogrojeh
Viroswa zhebka youndrena e kshepka
Viounce chongnie zhebkown jardek nieborzher
Chongnie e chongnie, vichongnondge nie morzheh.

Szavowal jardek na pomost babchown
'Ya swapiown zhebkown, tay za mniay zwap shiown'
E biednie jardek zz babchong niebogong
Chongno e chongno, vichongnondge nie mogong.

Figure 6.1 lists are some key words from the rhyme; the last three are to help you continue with more verses of the rhyme with children in your setting.

English word	Polish word	Pronunciation
Grandad	dziadek	jardek
Turnip	rzepka	zhebka
Grandma	babcia	babcha
To pull	ciągnąć	chongnonge
Grandson	wnuczek	vnucheck
Dog	Pies	peeyes
Cat	Kot	kot

Figure 6.1 'The Enormous Turnip': Polish and English vocabulary

* Author's note: I have been visiting Poland for sixteen years and know a number of words and some sentences. This is my own phonetic transcription. When I read my transcription of the Polish pronunciation to a Polish visitor, he could understand. However, these phonetics have been written to my accent. It makes you realise how difficult phonics and matching correct sounds can be! (AB)

Metalinguistic awareness

It is valuable to promote young children's metalinguistic awareness – their understanding of how language works. They are already showing implicit knowledge about this as they use language from day to day, but this can be heightened through talking and exploring language. In this chapter we have given examples of how song, rhyme and story all contribute to this, but here we will also consider examples of young children noticing aspects of accent and dialect and of how to play with words through humour.

Accent and dialect

Accent demotes the way language is pronounced. Dialect demotes the way language is used, and includes vocabulary, grammar and pronunciation.

> Cameron at age 3 is already noticing differences in dialect and pronunciation in the people around him. 'Why do you call them buks [books], Grandma – Mummy calls them books?' 'Why do you say wash the pots – Mummy says do the dishes?'

This shows how keenly children listen to language and can begin to notice similarities and differences, commencing analysis of language and metalinguistic awareness.

Alliteration

You can use alphabet songbooks to promote learning the alphabet in a kinaesthetic way through singing the words and miming to the actions of the song: Ants on the apple, Bats are bouncing. Many of the sentences are alliterative, with the same first letter of the word repeated. Draw children's attention to alliteration and repetitive sounds through songs and rhymes. Sing sentences that incorporate the children's names and what they like doing. For example: 'Shula sang a song of sixpence, song of sixpence, song of sixpence; Shula sang a song of sixpence on a sunny day.'

Humour

Children develop an understanding of humour and jokes from quite a young age. As they manipulate the language for fun and to tell a joke, they are demonstrating their metalinguistic awareness. Humour is part of normal conversation. Did you know that children laugh hundreds of times in a day whereas most adults are lucky if they laugh a few times? Children's humour can be completely different from adults. Silly words or phrases, gestures, use of intonation, pronunciation and tone of voice can signal or be part of a joke. Of course children don't always get the humour right and they will often roll about laughing at something that they've created; they can laugh at the silliest things and adults often don't get the joke!

The boys love telling jokes around the dinner table. Often they are knock-knock jokes like Dr Who? Or Jumbo. Stephan age 3, tries to make up his own using the same formula, but it is not always funny – e.g. what do you get if you cross a jacket and a jumper – answer – a jacket and a jumper. He uses things around him that he can see, to be the object of humour. He copies jokes his older brother tells.

Kirsten, at age 2, was already developing an understanding of humour. When her mum asked 'What's your name?' she replied 'It's Georgina. It's Sarah. It's Barbara' [names of children and adult friends]. Mum replied 'It's not', which leads to Kirsten giggling profusely and scrunching up her shoulders in delight.

Toilet humour is very popular with young children – probably from the age of 4. Nathan would go into fits of giggles when using words such as 'poopoobox'. Was he collecting such phrases as this at pre-school? He was definitely bringing it home to share with his parents, who were not always amused. Similarly Charlie and Adam often entertained themselves at mealtimes with anecdotes about bottoms or calling each other or one of the adults 'poo head'. They often sing songs about 'poo' or about someone going to the toilet. They evidently enjoy being risqué and naughty.

Playing with words

Playing with words helps children to recognise rhymes, letter sounds and shapes, and to hear sounds to make up words. Encourage parents to play games such as 'I spy', 'Simple Simon' or guess the missing word in a rhyme, or play games changing one letter – pin-tin-fin-fan-far-fat – for rhyme or alliteration to help them to develop early phonemic awareness (Fisher & Williams, 2004). Play:

> I went to market and I bought a sock, clock, rock, block
> I went to market and I bought a cat, hat, bat, rat
> I went to market and I bought a pen, hen, den.

Create boxes of objects beginning with the same letter – spade, sausage, shampoo, scissors, spider – to help contextualise it for the children. Play matching games that involve listening:

> 'I'm going to choose something that begins with a sound and if you choose something with the same sound you can put it on my tray.' This practitioner was promoting initial letter sounds through providing lots of objects and also playing Kim's game by encouraging the selection of objects from a tray. The children were at the very beginning of hearing the sounds and lots of support and repetition was needed. Although nursery was really noisy, the children were absolutely engaged and participating in the 'game'.

It is important to decide whether children are engaged and interested, if they are learning and developing knowledge of sounds easily. Children need a thorough grounding in music, rhyme, song and sound experiences before they have any formal focusing on phonic activities.

Early phonemic awareness

Language development continues after children have started school, as they are still acquiring vocabulary and learning how to pronounce words and gain understanding of their meanings. Bilingual support can ensure that children hear words in both languages. Young children who have language delay will also need lots of time for talking and will need to be supported through prompting and repetition. As acknowledged in the principles of the EYFS, young children are learning through different ways and at different rates. Both enough time and lots of active experiences are important for developing early phonemic awareness.

A foundation stage teacher uses spoken dialogues to encourage her children to use the whole range of pitch, stress and intonation with their voices to create a variety of sounds and so develop early phonemic awareness.

> Have you brought your talking voice?
> Yes, I've brought my talking voice.
> Have you brought your funny voice?
> Yes, I've brought my funny voice.

The children are encouraged to enjoy singing at different levels of high and low, exploring emotions of happy and sad, accents of posh and funny. Learning sounds are connected to movements and gestures and to be as kinaesthetic and multisensory as possible in fun ways:

- Ball bouncing – boing, boing, boing
- Wheeee – going down the slide
- Sssss snakes hisssssssing, going over and under
- Sh sh sh with finger
- Old man legs aching – ay, ay, ay.

Phonics

English is a very difficult language to learn to read. It is not a straightforward process because of the irregularities in the way phonemes are grouped to spell words. Children are able to start to read without knowing any letter sounds or names, but there is evidence to show that early capability with rhyme and alliteration is related to better success in reading at school. Goswami and Bryant (1990) found that children were able to handle syllables, rhyme and alliteration with confidence. They stressed the importance of phonological awareness in children's literacy development.

There is a concern that imposing phonics work on 4-year-olds can be detrimental to their overall language development. It is considered that a move to a strong emphasis on synthetic phonics could be at the expense of a whole language approach, which takes account of all the early language and literacy experiences discussed in this book. There is a worry that children will be encouraged to represent phonetically regular sounds that are at the expense them making meaning. Here are two teachers who think phonemic development is very important for learning to read, but they have different opinions about when and at what speed to teach phonics. They teach in quite different schools and are both very aware of their children's needs.

> I used to teach my reception class the 26 letter sounds. I'd let the children have a go at spelling and not correct them. Then I went on a Jolly Phonics course. The teacher had been teaching the 46 sounds and showed us a video on how the children were using them. It looked very good, so I decided to have a go and taught my class all the sounds after the Christmas holidays. They learnt the alphabet song with the actions, but once they'd learnt the sound they would no longer do the actions. However, if they got stuck you could see them mime the actions to help them remember the sound. They were using the kinaesthetic strategies in their learning. The children then began to use the phonics they acquired in their writing and that was the best thing. They could now spell 'sail'. They knew the 'ai' sound and could apply it. I used Jolly Phonics in conjunction with all the other strategies of story, reading, games, emergent writing etc. and have now turned from a sceptic into an advocate. [Reception teacher.]

> Ninety-nine per cent of the children in our Foundation Stage Unit are learning English as an additional language. I'm worried about them doing the synthetic phonics. They can get the 26 alphabet letter sounds plus ch/th/sh, but then there are 15 more phonemes that are quite complicated – vowel and consonant diagraphs – double ff, zz, ll, ng, oo, ou, ai, au, ee, ae, ir, qu. It gets more horrendous when they have to acquire igh, ear, ow, ur, plus a hundred high frequency words. Talk about pressurised and for whom – children or adults or both! We are supposed to do Phase 4 by the end of Reception. Children who are not 5 until the end of the school year are expected to compete with children who are 5 at the beginning of the school year – 11 months difference! [Foundation Stage teacher]

Synthetic phonics

The DfES book *Letters and Sounds* (2007b) describes what is required in Phase 1 (the first six weeks), which is advised to be done before children enter a reception class. Many of these are appropriate early years activities. Young children need to recognise and name the sounds they hear in their environment. Going on a listening walk, both indoors and outdoors, is a good activity to do with a small group. Playing sound lotto from a tape is useful for a guessing game, but be aware that there are some noises children might not be familiar with – for example will they recognise a brush, saw, wind or fire? This reception teacher describes how some children need a lot of exposure to environmental sounds, which is required in Phase One of *Letters and Sounds*:

> The children have to know environmental sounds. That means to be able to distinguish sounds, as well as know rhyme and alliteration. Second language learners sometimes have difficulty with the rhyming and also hearing the language in the environment. They are still learning the words and are concentrating on the meaning rather than on the sounds. We play lots of games and listen to tapes, yet they are still not able to discriminate some of the sounds and so need a lot of exposure to them. You need to be sure they have both enough maturity and experience to acquire them. [Reception teacher]

It is very useful to have knowledge about 'phonics' and to be able to articulate this to colleagues. The advice in *Letters and Sounds* is that you should know how to blend and segment clearly yourself, so that you can ensure that you are doing this correctly with children. Teach children the sound code systematically, so they do not have to guess it for themselves. *Letters and Sounds* will give you both definitions and how to teach phonics through modelling and getting children to practise. Recognising diagraphs and trigraphs takes time and children need plenty of opportunities to play and practise them.

Linguistic phonics

Linguistic phonics (McEvoy and Greer, 2007) places emphasis on developing oral language during children's first year at school through focusing on spoken language, developing attention and listening, and phonological awareness. The stages of linguistic phonics have been developed with speech and language therapists who have no doubt about the value of oral language development. The starting point is speech and children are encouraged to listen to the sounds they say and then learn how they are represented in their own spoken language. The pace is fast and children discover through context that the same sound can be represented in different ways through series of experiences. They are offered a wide range of books, not just phonetically 'decodable' books, and learn book-handling skills and the enjoyment of stories with supportive adults, who model reading, fluency, expression and encouraging discussion about the story.

So with all this advice and differences in opinion about the teaching of phonics, what do you need to promote? This chapter should have provided you with ideas in how to make your setting a rich environment:

• Music and sound
• Songs and singing
• Rhyme and rhythm

- Talk about sounds
- Play with words
- Lots of listening to stories and love of books
- Storying and rhyming
- Contextualisation through everyday activities and play experiences
- Letter recognition through matching to environmental print in real life
- A developing metalinguistic awareness – talking about language
- Onomatopoeia – playing with sounds

 Questions for reflection and discussion

- Do you feel comfortable to sing with children?
- Have you a broad repertoire of songs, rhymes, music activities and sound games?
- Can you talk with confidence to parents about the value of rhyme, rhythm, sound and song?
- Are you able to understand the different perspectives about teaching phonics?

 Key points for practice

- Children are naturally disposed to rhythm and movement, which should be capitalised upon in activities.
- Rhyme, rhythm, sound and song are important for developing young children's language and literacy skills.
- Practitioners should offer these through playful multisensory activities that encourage enthusiasm and enjoyment.
- Playing with sounds through different activities helps phonemic development.
- Phonic learning situations should be purposeful and meaningful for children.
- Determine children's individual needs about what is appropriate for their phonological development.

Further Reading

DfES (2007a) *Early Years Foundation Stage*. London: DfES.
DfES (2007b) *Letters and Sounds: Principles and Practice of High Quality Phonics*. London: DfES.
Lewis, M. and Ellis, S. (2006) *Phonics*. London: PCP.

 Useful websites

www.talktoyourbaby.org.uk
www.education.ex.ac.uk/music-one2one
http://www.bigeyedowl.co.uk/songs.htm
http://www.bbc.co.uk/parenting/play_and_do/babies_songs.shtml
http://www.standards.dfes.gov.uk/phonics/

7

Emerging Literacy: Playful Reading and Writing

 Learning objectives

Acquiring literacy is crucial for children's educational achievement and this should be promoted through a wide range of activities and experiences from the very early years. This chapter presents what skills, knowledge and attitudes are needed to achieve competence. We explain why it is important to promote these through playful experiences, taking care not to push children, particularly boys, too rapidly through prescriptive activities. We will explore the relevance of environmental print that surrounds young children and how practitioners and parents can use this to promote a curiosity and desire to find out more. Ideas from promoting literacy through role-play and meaningful contextualised experience are also included in this chapter. We look at:

- What is emergent literacy?
- How reading and writing can be fun.
- What resources are available.

So, what have the previous six chapters told you about communication, language and literacy in the Early Years Foundation Stage? You should hopefully be replying that children need a multitude of experiences of oral language, of talking, listening, storying, rhyming, reading and singing. These are the building blocks of literacy and make the difference as to how quickly and easily they acquire reading and writing. If children have not had this multitude of experiences there can be problems with language delay, which is becoming more prevalent in young children (Potter, 2007). If this is the case for any young children entering your setting, then you must promote and provide these experiences. Chapter 5 demonstrated how important it is to encourage children to listen to stories and develop an interest in books and reading, and this is something you cannot start too soon. This concluding chapter looks at how children become literate, how they take ownership of language and begin to become effective communicators. Our job as early years practitioners is to promote an enthusiasm for reading and writing.

Some children are not always ready for formal literacy experiences and may find sitting down at a table for sustained periods difficult. This may be due to their abundance of energy, limited fine motor control, or just a desire to do something more interesting or appropriate than the adults might be offering. Motivating young children to want to learn to read and write is the route to achievement. Early literacy experiences need to be fun and easily acquired. Most other European countries do not promote formal literacy experiences with young children until they are at least 6 or even 7 years old! They then normally find that their children acquire both reading and writing with little difficulty. Young children are actively pre-programmed to learn, but just because they can learn and gain mastery of formal literacy activities, does not necessarily mean we should be teaching them at a very young age. This chapter therefore addresses literacy through an emergent approach and discusses how complicated literacy can be. How can you make literacy acquisition meaningful and exciting for the young children in your care?

Early Years Foundation Stage and literacy

Fifty per cent of the early learning goals in the EYFS are directly related to literacy. It may seem to you that this book is unbalanced and that 50 per cent of these chapters need to be directly linked to literacy! There is no doubt in our minds that many of the ideas discussed in this book ultimately contribute towards early literacy. Early language foundations need to be firmly established for adequate and easy literacy acquisition to occur. Without children getting a multitude of oral language, story, rhyming and song experiences, the route to literacy will be much more difficult than it needs to be. These essential components of becoming literate are all important and whilst for some children one individual component might take a priority in how they acquire reading and writing, for others it will have less importance. It is absolutely fundamental to children's acquisitions of early literacy that you can offer a balanced diet of experiences in order to maximise the ways each child can learn to read and write. You need to have a good knowledge and understanding of the reading and writing processes and how to foster a range of experiences so that every child can fulfil his or her potential.

The following expectations for the early learning goals in the EYFS (DfES, 2007a) for literacy acquisition have been addressed in Chapters 5 and 6 through the promotion of story, storying and book experiences and encountering rhyming, sound and song:

- Link sounds to letters, naming and sounding the letters of the alphabet
- Use phonic knowledge to write simple regular words and make phonetically plausible attempts at more complex words
- Explore and experiment with sounds, words and texts
- Retell narratives in the correct sequence, drawing on language patterns of stories
- Read a range of familiar and common words and simple sentences independently
- Know that print carries meaning and, in English, is read from left to right and top to bottom
- Show an understanding of the elements of stories, such as main character, sequence of events and openings, and how information can be found in non-fiction texts to answer questions about where, who, why and how (DfES, 2007)

This chapter will further develop these EYFS expectations and will introduce methods and activities for promoting the following three early learning goals that focus on writing:

- Attempt writing for different purposes, using features of different forms such as lists, stories and instructions
- Write their own names and other things such as labels and captions, and begin to form simple sentences, sometimes using punctuation
- Use a pencil and hold it effectively to form recognisable letters, most of which are correctly formed (DfES, 2007a)

What is emergent literacy?

The term 'emergent literacy' was first introduced by Marie Clay in 1966 and gradually replaced the notion of 'pre-reading' (Riley, 2006). As noted throughout this book, children will acquire language and literacy skills from their earliest years. Most children cannot escape literacy; it permeates their environment – in their home, in nursery, on the television, in supermarkets and in the high street. Signs and notices in our highly literate environment surround us, even if literacy does not have a high profile at home and parents do not read books or newspapers. All young children will have a number of everyday experiences with literacy. They will have received birthday cards, visited a favourite restaurant, chosen sweets, observed electronic signs and digital screens, looked through catalogues, scribbled on pictures, held tickets and receipts on excursions. They enter school with familiarity of literacy; what varies for each child is the quality of interaction with these experiences.

As an adult do you model literacy for children? Do they see you:

- Enjoying reading and writing?
- Reading to yourself?
- Reading different items: poems, books, stories, messages, newspapers, instructions, advertisements?
- Writing for a range of purposes: notes, letters, lists, invitations, diary entries, filling in forms?
- Commenting on your reading and writing?

As a student teacher in the 1970s, I would worry about children's 'reading readiness' and how would I discover the moment they were ready to read? How would I know when to introduce them to phonics or books?

Can see how ironic this comment is, bearing in mind what you've found out in this book so far?

How did you learn to read?

Reading should be a pleasure; a love of the written word can take you into stories both real and fantasy, into someone else's thoughts and ideas, so that your own world is expanded and enriched. Cast your mind back, can you remember how you learnt to read? If you learned easily then you might only remember the names of books or characters in the reading scheme that your school used. However, if you had difficulty and struggled you may have recollections like JJ. He moved from Glasgow to Ormskirk in Lancashire at the age of 5. Although already reading successfully at home, he was making no progress in school due to misunderstandings about accent and dialect. JJ stood in line at the teacher's desk listening to the other children read and when it was his turn he imitated their Lancashire 'thees' and thous', getting confused about the whole process! In another example, a teacher on an in-service course remembers that she struggled and learnt through smacking words: if you did not read the words written on the blackboard correctly – you got smacked! Sue Townsend, author of *The Diary of Adrian Mole*, was 8 years old before she learnt to read. She had a teacher like a 'dyspeptic badger' who obviously didn't engage with Sue's learning needs effectively. Sue eventually taught herself to read, when she was at home with a spectacular case of mumps and her mother brought home some 'William' books from a rummage sale. Sue records how the squiggles became words, the words became sentences and then – lo and behold – she began to read (Townsend, in Fraser, 1992).

A multisensory approach to reading

Reading is a complicated process and involves a wide range of skills. Children need active and varied experiences to help master the complex skills. They need to achieve through experience and success, as failure can lead to frustration and cause barriers to learning.

 Jenny and Harry

The first word that Jenny learnt to read and spell at age 2 years 6 months 'BUM' taught to her by her dad; it was their shared joke. Already she could write her name and read some words. However, her 4-year-old cousin, Harry, when asked 'How do you write your name?' replied 'I don't know; you do a stick down like that'. He did not see the purpose or need to write. Both these children have similar lifestyles and yet their interests are completely different. Jenny loves to read and write, but Harry is not yet interested in sitting down to literacy activites. But when Harry spent a full day at the National Railway Museum in York, he was fully engrossed in exploring and examining the trains and other exhibits, asking questions, getting on board and pretending to drive the Mallard and the Rocket. He read timetables with his Granddad, interacting all day with both people and exhibits. Here he was busy, engrossed and absorbed; engaged in listening, questioning and even reading.

You need to cue into children's interests and play experiences and help them create their interest and need for literacy. 'Children learn how to make literacy their own invention, in similar ways as that they previously learned to do with spoken language' (Riley, 2006: 49). Remember the following concepts introduced in Chapter 1 with regard to language acquisition?

- Phonology – grapho-phonemic cues (letter/sound correspondence)
- Semantics (meanings)
- Syntax and knowledge of sentence structure (grammar)

These are also key to learning to read, along with other crucial aspects for early language development, also introduced in Chapter 1:

- Previous experience, background knowledge and cultural experiences are important
- Repetition and practice of words, phrases and structures
- Knowledge of how language works, that is, all that children have intuitively acquired through hearing and using language

Children try to make sense of their world and the learning process by using all strategies available and this is the same for reading as for everything else they learn. Widen their repertoire by relating everything to previous experience and help to make connections, scaffolding their knowledge. Children need to be interested, to be motivated and learn to achieve through building on early success. When reading with children:

- Give them time to think, look and re-read for themselves
- Support by introducing the book – title, characters, content
- Encourage them to use a variety of clues – if one doesn't work try another
- Encourage them to think 'Does that look right?', 'Does that sound right?', 'Does that make sense?'

While still building on their knowledge of oral language, stories, books and phonics, children will make sense of the reading process through using the following cuing systems:

Grapho-phonic (letters and sounds)

- Trying to find patterns in the print
- Sounding out words or parts of words using phonics
- Discovering that sounds are important for making sense of the text

Semantic (meaning)

- Looking at pictures – interpreting them in different ways
- Guessing words from context and revising the guess as more of the meaning is revealed
- Filling in words to 'make meaning' of the sentence
- Returning to previous part of the text
- Using knowledge of traditional stories

Syntactic (grammar)

- Using knowledge of word order in sentences
- Using knowledge of word endings and their grammatical functions
- Using knowledge of 'function words' and their grammatical purposes

Social

- Seeking confirmation from others
- Repeating each other's utterances
- Discussing what it might mean
- Discussing the picture and testing out hypotheses

Through listening to emergent readers making sense of text and reading, the strategies brought to the reading process can be observed. See how Akfa and Mykelti's reading processes are developing:

 Akfa, aged 4 years 1 month

Akfa chose a book from the bookcase and demanded that I listened to her telling me the story. She liked to have an audience. She demonstrated knowledge of how a book works; that the text told a story to be read and listened to, the text continued from page to page in order, that the illustrations held meaning and related to the text on the page. She used her voice with emphasis and stress, showing how stories should be read. Her reading was very interesting and she demonstrated her confidence as an emergent reader. She placed an emphasis on using the definite article before the nouns observed in the illustrations:

The baby, the chair.
The baby, the mummy.
The baby, the pram.
The baby, the baby, the baby.
The baby, the dinner.

 Mykelti, aged 5 years 8 months

Mykelti read *The Red Hen and the Sly Fox* with competence. He had chosen a book that he enjoys reading and used intonation to support the telling of the story. He self-corrects and double checks, re-reading proper names to make sure if is correct, only occasionally using the illustrations as cues. Mykelti uses:

- grapho-phonic cues using a substitute beginning or ending with the same letter: here–high; will–went; put–pit
- semantic cues using a meaning substitute: home–house; this–the; says–said
- syntactical cues using a grammatical substitute in the form of a similar verb, adverb, preposition or noun: there–this; go–get; looks–looked

Mykelti often uses a combination of cues as the semantic, syntactical and graphophonic overlap. He uses pre-knowledge of the story to read difficult words such as 'dizzy' and 'splashes' and uses picture cues when he cannot recognise the word: e.g. 'down', 'bag'. Occasionally he asks the adult for help when he has difficulty that affects his reading and understanding of the text. He reads for meaning and enjoyment. At the end of the book he chatted about the content of the story and expressed opinions of what happened to the main protagonists.

Guiding readers

You should read with children through a shared process as the closeness of reading with an adult is special. Ensure you read with and talk to children about the text. Do not treat it as a test where you continually correct them, but guide them to undertanding and success. Encourage them to:

- Make sense of the whole text
- Make connections to familiar experiences
- Talk about and understand what you are reading
- Ask questions about the reading process
- See patterns in words and letters
- Gain visual images of words
- Use illustrations to help meaning
- Match pictures to words

Throughout the reading process demonstrate:

- Page or book layout
- Left to right orientation
- Turning the page in different directions
- Scanning backwards and forwards for cues
- How texts and stories work
- Punctuation and what it's for

Have you ever been in the situation that Danielle finds herself in as she reads *Jack and the Beanstalk* with Gus, aged 4 (who, by the way, has a broad Yorkshire accent)? What are your thoughts on this scenario? What, in your opinion, are the positives and negatives?

 Danielle and Gus

D: What do you remember about the book?
G: He fell down and hurt him.
D: How did he stop the giant?
G: He chopped it.
D: He managed to save the hen though, what do you think he did with the hen?

> G: He could eat 'em. He could have them for his tea. He could chuck 'em at winders.
>
> D: But isn't that naughty?
>
> G: Yeah, car winders. When I was a baby we had a blue car and I smashed it on winder. I can pick car up, I can even pick cooker up me, reyt up thear. I was strong but I'm not now.
>
> D: Have you got anything in your garden that looks like a beanstalk?
>
> G: Yeah, a tree and I can get an axe and chop. It would fall over and smash and it'd break that uver house. When I war a boy I could climb up it and I bet I could pick it up. I can even pick that table up.
>
> D: What did Jack do?
>
> G: OK, you know that fish in that tank it war a shark and me dad and me had catch it in the big boat.
>
> D: Really, did you go fishing with your dad?
>
> G: Yeah and that shark it eat boat an we war in water and that boatlife came.
>
> D: Boatlife? Oh lifeboat. Did the lifeboat take you home?
>
> G: Yeah, but that shark tried to get us and we went faster and faster, but it didn't get us.
>
> D: Oh dear, that sounds like it was scary.
>
> G: I want scared. I can fight that shark; I am strong me.
>
> D: Well I think you are very brave.
>
> G: Can we go and see if they've smashed that Ferrari?
>
> D: OK then, thank you for reading with me, it's been lots of fun.

Did you find this scenario amusing? What was Gus concerned with? How lively is his oral language and vivid is his imagination? Who is in control? Who is the superhero in the story and what is the connection to Jack and the Beanstalk? How would you capitalise on this scenario? Gus is obviously quite assertive and confident and in his imagination he is strong and brave like Jack and, at this moment, this is more exciting for him than reading the story. Danielle keeps trying to get him to return to talking about the story but although he is polite and answers her, he then returns to another of his own stories. This shows you that you can miss all the wonderful (if violent!) imaginative storying if you are more focused on completing a task than listening to the child. Think about questioning, how to make connections to the story and how to make literacy more exciting for the child. Perhaps Gus in this case could be encouraged to draw or make models of his own story, you could scribe it for him to read or record it for listening and retelling.

You need to:

- Model reading and apprenticeship children into reading
- Talk with children about stories, books and reading
- Develop children's awareness of sounds
- Value the knowledge and culture that children have

Within the Primary National Strategy (PNS) the model of 'simple view of reading' demonstrates how important it is for children to have both word recognition and language comprehension to gain reading comprehension. A diagram with four quadrants enables teachers to easily place where their assessments of each child's capabilities lie. It is important that children have lively and interactive phonic experiences, as discussed in Chapter 6.

The writing process – what is involved in writing?

There is a lot involved in the writing process and the conventions and skills include composition and transcription.

In **composition**:

- Ideas and thoughts
- A purpose for writing
- Planning and organising the writing
- Vocabulary: nouns, adjectives, verbs, adverbs, prepositions, clauses etc.
- Drafting
- Structure of text
- Making sense and cohesion: clarity of thought and writing

In **transcription**:

- Fine motor control with a writing implement
- Directionality: left to right, top to bottom (in English)
- Handwriting skills
- Letter formation
- Spaces between words
- Sentence structure
- Spelling
- Punctuation
- Usage of correct tenses
- Layout

Vygotsky stated that writing is one of the most abstract things we have to do. The EYFS requests that you provide opportunities for the children to:

- See adults writing
- Experiment with writing for themselves through making marks, personal writing symbols and conventional script
- Become aware of languages and writing systems other than English and communication systems such as signing and Braille [DfES, 2007a].

Encouraging fine motor control for writing

If children do not have gross motor skills such as arm circling and jumping they will definitely find it difficult to coordinate between their fingers and pencils. Activities to improve fine motor control include: drawing and colouring, building with Lego,

Look at me, I'm writing

play-dough and clay modelling, cutting, threading beads, sewing. Children can also trace their finger over shapes, in the sand or cornflour, write letters in the air and other kinaes-thetic activities. Pattern-making from left to right is helpful. Most children will have handled writing and drawing implements from 18 months old. One of Jacqui's early attempts at writing was with red crayon on the wallpaper above her cot in the bedroom! Chloe used her mother's lipstick on the kitchen wall.

The successful way to hold a pencil is with the tips of the thumb and forefinger in contact with the pencil with the middle finger supporting from below with the barrel of the instrument resting against the bottom of the index finger. It is helpful to have the paper at a slight angle. A way to help left-handed writers is to get the child to sit with the elbow close to the body with the paper to the left side angled slightly to the right. Lateralisation, left or right-handedness, develops after a child's second year, so allow young children to select their preference. It is useful to capitalise on children's physical experiences to develop writing movements, hand and eye co-ordination that will help children with their handwriting. 'Write Dance' is an approach that encourages children to feel, hear and experience what letters are like, through movement, sound, song, rhyme, games and music experiences, before they actually begin to write them. Children should be encouraged to scribble, doodle, circle, experience and experiment in varied ways and so develop self-confidence in handling writing implements.

Involving parents in children's emergent literacy

Children will make much better progress when parents support their children's emergent literacy. These early experiences make such a difference to children's later achievements. Encourage parents to read and write with their children at home and advocate them supporting and being part of their children's literacy development. However, do advise against over-pressurising and that the child's enjoyment and motivation are of high importance. You could think about organising literacy workshops for parents or invite them in to support and be part of children's learning through play. In the Sheffield 'Early Literacy Development Project', Weinburger et al. (1990) developed a collaborative project with parents that concentrated on pre-school literacy. The project concentrated on environmental print, shared reading and shared writing. Parents were encouraged to model reading (e.g. a newspaper) and writing (e.g. shopping lists) to provide literacy materials and to encourage success in non-conventional forms (e.g. invented spellings). The project found that parents became much more supportive of their children's literacy.

Parents can be advised to:

- Share shopping lists, menus, recipes, notices
- Draw attention to and write names of family and friends
- Point out signs and labels in the supermarket, on posters, on buses and in the street
- Match their child's name and initial letter sound to letters in other words
- Involve their child regularly in a variety of reading material around the home and encourage children's responses to text
- Model reading and writing and 'apprentice' their child into literacy
- Make time to share and have fun with stories and books
- Engage in shared reading of books and encourage prediction, picture cues, discussion about stories and texts
- Write postcards, emails, texts with children
- Recognise children's early literacy achievements through praise and encouragement

Parents can make literacy interesting for children through everyday experiences at home. The following scenario is one such example:

 Todd, age 3 years

The cat had been hiding behind the settee all morning and would not come out. Overhearing his older brother being asked to write a note for the two boys next door to come to lunch, Todd had the idea to leave the cat a note to tell her to come out so he could stroke her. The 3-year-old began to write his name in large letters on a piece of paper and, assisted by an adult, learnt how to write a word that was new to him – cat.

J: Are you writing a note to the cat?
T: So we go. Down, cross, round, up down, up down.
J: That's excellent, isn't it?

J: It's a curly c. Excellent. That's it.

T: Just like the 'o'?

J: Well, it shouldn't close at the end. Shall I write it and you copy? We have to do it here, so do a curly 'c', so that's a round but you don't close it. Then an 'a', which is another round and a stick, and then a 't' is 't' is like Todd, isn't it? Like that. Do you want to try it? Do a round.

T: Round.

J: A round. Yes, and don't close it. And then another round. That one's completely round and then a little stick. That's it, and then a 't' for Todd. Excellent! Aren't you clever? You've written cat there, haven't you? Clever boy! Are you going to show the cat?

T: Yes.

Todd took the finished letter and placed it just behind the settee where the cat was hiding. The group then went out for a walk to the park. After going to the park, Todd rushed into the front room to see what had happened. When he opened the door to find the cat (albeit a different cat) sitting on the sofa waiting for his return, he was incredulous. He went round and told everyone his letter had worked. His eyes were sparkling with surprise and intrigue. For Todd, it was like magic!

It is also important that you value the ways different cultures learn literacy and to make yourself aware of the differences. For example, rote learning is promoted in Islamic Madrassas and children attending these schools may find learning by rote a valuable way into literacy. Other families may not value and understand the appropriacy of emergent writing supported in early years settings and prefer their children to form fully formed letters and words. Gregory (1997) advocates that we need to capitalise on family experience and expectations and to recognise the knowledge held by family members as mediators of the home language and culture to the children. Parents can help in enabling children to translate words in both languages, and you should advise parents who cannot read English themselves that they can still help in exactly the same ways as were stated in the list on page 108. It is just as valuable to model reading and writing in Urdu, Polish or Swahili and to encourage children to develop emergent literacy in more than one language.

Role-play and emergent writing

Do you find that you never seem to be off duty, even on holiday, and that you look for resources that can be used in your activities with children – whether it is shells from the seashore, pine cones from a forest or interesting objects from souvenir shops? It was on one such occasion, holidaying in Filey, that the three chicks and the Grasper were acquired and their story emerged. Their purpose was to inspire 5-year-olds to become willingly and enthusiastically engaged in emergent writing. The characters were to stimulate the children to become letter writers, to engage in a two-way correspondence: receiving letters with news can be exciting, particularly when it is personalised.

First, the story of 'The Three Chicks' was introduced to the children. You will note that it has many resemblances to the *Three Little Pigs*, a traditional story that is not only valuable for its anticipation and excitement, and its repetitive storylines that children can easily predict and join in with, but is also a super springboard for topics on materials or forces. However, it is not particularly suitable to focus a lengthy topic on this story about pigs if your group contains Muslim children. So instead of pigs there were chicks and instead of a wolf, there was the 'Grasper' – the greedy, growling, grumpy, grizzly Grasper. As you will see in this story, it is so useful to maximise alliteration wherever possible! The following story and a miniature role-play landscape were introduced to children in a reception class.

> Once up on a time, there lived three little chicks: Charlie Chick, Cherry Chick and Choy Chick. They lived happily in the castle with their parents, King Cockrell and Queen Hen, until the day came when they grew up and needed to leave home. Their Majesties gave each of the chicks ten gold coins and they were told to build their own houses. Charlie Chick left the castle first by the right hand path. At the bottom of the hill in the village he met a dog lying down calling 'Straw for sale, straw for sale, only four gold coins!' 'Cool!' said Charlie Chick, 'if I build my house of straw, I will have six gold coins left to buy a Transformer'. So he bought the straw and built his house. Cherry Chick was the next to leave the castle and she went down the left hand path of the hill and met a dog sitting down who was calling 'Sticks for sale, sticks for sale, only seven gold coins.' 'Brill!' said Cherry Chick. 'If I build my house of sticks, I will have three gold coins left to buy chocolate.' So she bought the sticks and built her house. Finally, Choy Chick left the castle and climbed down the middle road on the hill, where at the bottom in the village, she met a dog, standing up, selling bricks. 'Bricks for sale, bricks for sale, only 10 gold coins.' 'Fantastic!' said Choy Chick. 'I'll build my house of bricks.' All three chicks lived very happily in their houses, until one day the Grasper came to the village. He stood on the edge of the village and shouted at the top of his voice – 'Where are you chicks? My tummy is grumbling. I'll grease your bones. I'll grind you to pieces. I'll grab you from your houses.' The three chicks shivered inside their houses and wondered if they were safe from the Grasper.

This story can be substituted with any characters and be made meaningful to children's own experiences. The importance of this is to select key aspects and contextualise to the children's activities. It is important for you to decide where and how to take the story and to be flexible enough to let the children do the directing. The story was told and finished at the point where the Grasper arrived, to encourage the children to think about problems and resolutions. They drew on their knowledge and experience of the Three Little Pigs story about what might happen next.

The children played with the role-play landscape of hill, paths, houses and characters. They retold the story and recreated their own. Then, a few days later, a letter from the Grasper was found in the classroom. (Remember – a key objective of the story was to encourage the children to become letter writers.) He had just arrived in the area and was extremely hungry and could the children tell him where he could get any chickens. The class listened to the letter and then decided not to help the Grasper. Fortunately (because otherwise where would the story have gone next?), Andrew stood up and declared to the class that not everyone is a vegetarian and that most of us really needed to eat meat. It was amazing how his oratory took effect. The majority of the class decided they would help the Grasper and they wrote replies saying how he could get the chickens. Rory told him to blow down the houses; Sadika and Nadia made him a disguise, so that he could pretend to be Red Riding Hood and capture the chickens, Paris directed them to Boggis' hen house Number 1 (from Roald Dahl's *Fantastic Mr Fox* – these examples remind us again of how letter experiences permeate children's thinking). Nicklaus made a post-box and the children engaged in much letter writing to the Grasper. It was so useful to have to write only one letter back to all the children from the Grasper. It was however quite difficult to get my dog Kassie to sign the story with her mudded paw! There were lots of adventures and writing experiences during the next month: kidnappings, ransom letters and rescues; requests for building plans; directions, clues and instructions; recipes and menus.

It can be seen that already several aspects of the six areas of learning have been introduced and that there is a vast potential for cross-curricular work:

- Personal, social and emotional development: working collaboratively; promoting empathy; listening to others' points of view
- Communication, language and literacy: storying; writing and reading letters and instructions; problem solving discussions
- Number and reasoning: counting; number bonds; focus on '3'-ness; thrift and economics
- Knowledge and understanding of the world: forces; materials; landscapes; jobs; buildings; families
- Physical development: directions; positions; building and manipulating materials
- Creative development: role-play; drawing maps, designing buildings and costumes; story-making, painting, drawing and modelling

Other successful ideas

In another class a beanstalk (carpet tube) was growing from floor to ceiling with a pair of trouser legs and large laced-up boots dangling down from the top. This class corresponded with the giant and drew on knowledge of stories of Jack's, Jim's and Jasper's beanstalks. The children wrote him instructions, made him glasses and other adornments; blamed him for making the classroom untidy; asked for help in solving problems and told about important happenings in the children's lives.

After hearing about these two scenarios, one student commented that the children in her class were too 'streetwise' to be 'fooled' into writing to imaginary characters. However, she decided to give it a try and made 'wolf' prints that walked into her classroom. She was so excited when the children wholeheartedly became involved in the role-play, one saying she heard the leaves rustling on the way to school and another saying he could smell that a wolf had been in the room. They too got engaged in writing to the wolf. You need to be imaginative and inventive yourself and open the door for children to walk through into story worlds. Capitalise on what they are excited by and see how they can be motivated to further develop the story experiences and so become storywriters, correspondents, authors and philosophers.

Playful literacy

Developing emergent literacy in the role-play area occurs in most early years settings. However, when planning for these experiences, don't just think about the resources, but also think about the communication, language and literacy demands. The following should be fairly self-explanatory and through planning in this way, other adults can become more focused in how to scaffold children's experiences.

Railway station, trains and Eurostar
Initial stimulus: Stories, video, visit, guest visitor, artefact, children's or adult's own holidays, travel to stay with family, postcards, topic on journeys
Physical resources: Uniforms, ticket desk, information centre, tannoy, café area, passport control, numbered seats, brochures, globes, maps
Communication, language and literacy resources: Postcards and posters, luggage labels, passports (made by children), telephone, computer time-tables, tickets, destination information, newpaper shop, café menus, buffet trollies with signs
Literacy objectives: Speaking and listening – developing conversational skills through turn-taking, asking questions, characterisation, meeting people, visiting family Reading – destination information, signs, directions, numerical information, brochures Writing – producing labels, tickets, postcards, advertisements, creating passport with personal details, lists, tickets, signs, writing stories
Target vocabulary: Rains, railway station, Eurostar, driver, steward, luggage, travel, journey, destination, holiday, passport, tickets, information, noisy, busy, bustling, exciting, departure, arrival
Role-play language: What is your destination? Can I see your ticket please? What time does the train arrive? There has been a delay. Where is the platform? What time is it please? How long is the journey? How much will it cost? How many people are travelling?
Role of the adult(s): Model and initiate language and activities; build upon children's play; support sustained shared thinking with children; introduce new vocabulary and sentence structures; pose problems; get into role as a character; let children direct the play

Figure 7.1 Playful literacy at the railway station

You can encourage families to develop their own literacy and role-play experiences through the toys their children play with at home. One family made notices for Hayley's farm:

CHERRY TREE FARM	PRIMROSE COTTAGE	DAVIDSON'S DAIRY
Please shut the gate Milking Times are 8.00 a.m. Please don't feed the horse Watch out for trains NO SMOKING Beware of the Bull John's Job Rota 1. Milk the cows 2. Muck out the pigs 3. Feed the ducks 4. Drive the tractor 5. Ride the pony	5.00 p.m.	

New events or problems that needed resolving were introduced periodically into the children's play. An animal was ill and the vet was called; some sheep had escaped from a field; John was not doing his jobs; a storm caused some damage. The children were involved in writing letters, completing insurance forms, making lists, displaying notices. Literacy became part of their play and fun to do.

Final thoughts

This chapter has provided you with knowledge and understanding about early literacy development. In fact, that is what the whole book has been about – the importance of early language development. Young children become successful through enjoyable and meaningful experiences. Remember that communication, language and literacy should permeate your provision and Appendix 1 shows a plan of how to do this. We hope you will feel confident about employing some of the ideas and activities from this book in your own setting. Be inspired and encouraged to put them into practice! If in doubt, tell a story.

 Questions for reflection and discussion

- Consider how you can promote 'emergent literacy'?
- How can you model reading and writing for children in meaningful ways?
- How could you provide activities to promote children's emerging literacy skills?
- What do parents need to know about their children's literacy development?

 Key points for practice

- Reading and writing should be fun and you need to make it so for young children.
- Acquiring literacy is crucial for children's educational achievement.
- Model reading and writing in your setting.
- Reading and writing are complex skills that require lots of practice.
- Promote literacy through meaningful contextualised experiences.
- Do not push children into literacy activities that might hinder their motivation.

 Further Reading

Aldridge, M. (2003) *Meeting the Early Learning Goals through Role Play*. London: David Fulton.
Oussoren, R.A. (2005) *Write Dance in the Nursery*. London: PCP.
Riley, J. (2006) *Language and Literacy 3–7*. London: Sage.

 Useful websites

http://www.literacytrust.org.uk/Research/earlyindex.html
http://www.standards.dfes.gov.uk/primary
http://www.ncll.org.uk

Appendix 1 Theories of Language Acquisition

Behaviourist

The behaviourist view sees the processes of stimulus/response and imitation/reinforcement as the key factors in the acquisition of language. The association of an object with the word and the reinforcement provided by the adult when the child tries to say the word was one explanation. More complex language behaviour is said to result from an increasingly complicated pattern of response chaining. Clearly, some aspects of our first language are acquired through imitation and reinforcement or we would not acquire the sounds and the vocabulary of those around us. However, it is unlikely that language acquisition is such a simple process. While it is true that children appear to imitate some aspects of adult language, they seem to choose what and when to do so. Professor B. Skinner is the man most often associated with this view of language acquisition.

Nativist

Nativists criticised behaviourist accounts of language acquisition. They maintained that behaviourism could not explain the speed with which children acquired language, since most children have already acquired virtually the whole system by the age of 5 or 6. In addition, they asserted that it could not account for certain types of behaviour, for example, children at a certain stage seem to adopt a new rule and generalise it ('goed', 'sawed' etc.). They seem to use their own grammar rules and gradually enlarge their system as they develop. They are also resistant to correction if their current set of rules does not fit with the adult's. Nativists believe that we must be born with a language acquisition faculty of some sort. This has been called a language acquisition device or 'LAD'. The nature of this LAD, is the subject of some debate among nativists. Some believe it to be a specific 'human language faculty' which might contain the rules of a universal grammar and also procedures for responding to human language. This is the strong form of the theory. Some believe that the LAD is simply a set of faculties for processing experience in ways which are particularly appropriate to human language. In other words, the language faculty is part of a larger mental system. This is where the views of Nativists and Cognitive theorists may overlap. Professor N. Chomsky was a powerful figure in proposing a nativist view of language acquisition to counter that of the behaviourists.

Cognitive

Cognitive theorists are concerned with the intellect and how it develops. They see language as part of and dependent on the development of our thinking skills. Jean Piaget was a psychologist working in Geneva who developed the idea that our thinking follows a number of stages in each of the areas of our experience. He believed that our intellect grew as we interacted with and acted upon our environment. As our mental faculties develop, we come to acquire language as a symbol system to help us to code and communicate our perceptions and understandings. Language also, in Piaget's view, exposed us to how other people viewed the world and led to the need to negotiate or re-negotiate our understanding. Piaget believed, as do many cognitive theorists who are not followers of Piaget, that language is dependent on intellectual development. Vygotsky, a famous Russian psychologist who has many strong supporters, stresses the point that language and thinking processes must interact in order for intellectual development to go beyond the most primitive level. This is an important debate: does language follow behind thinking or must the two go hand-in-hand?

Interactionist

In recent years, researchers into language development have begun to stress far more than previously that the roots of language lie in the early attempts of infants and carers to interact and communicate with each other. For this reason, we have labelled them interactionists although the theorists who have contributed to this view come from many different backgrounds. They see the beginnings of language in early conversation; what is sometimes called 'proto-conversation'. Carers, usually mothers, in everyday routines and play, behave with infants as if they are taking part in conversations. Infants seem to be born with the propensity to be sociable. They pay particular attention to their carers and learn to respond, at first with face and body movements, later with gesture and intonation and ultimately with words. Carers provide a kind of scaffold in which the child can become familiar with routines of communication and can gradually take more initiative. When the child comes to use their first words, they fit readily into an established pattern of communication. Jerome Bruner and his associates have been instrumental in propagating this perspective.

Socio-culturalism

Socio-cultural theory was first established by Vygotsky and is connected closely to the history and culture of communities, including minority groups. Every community has distinctive characteristics defined through cultural practices, relationships, norms and expectations. Children develop their emotional attachments and social relationships, learning language and communication strategies through interacting with significant others. They learn through social situations, and their development evolves through being embedded in their immediate environment and society. Children's behaviour and understanding therefore occur within social relationships mediated by cultural practices, which are shaped by knowledge and beliefs about what is culturally expected. It can be seen that cross-cultural diversity – how adults and children interact – is crucial in the co-construction of learning and for ensuring equity for individual children, who will each have experienced particular cultural values within their personal families and communities. Adults need to examine their own cultural practices, expectations, communication strategies and how these affect their teaching and relationships with children – how they instruct, cue children into and scaffold their learning.

Appendix 2 Long-Term Planning: Early Years Unit

Continuous provision – literacy areas – indoors and outdoors

Key Learning Opportunities

- To share, empathise, respect and listen to others' ideas through story and role-play experiences
- To extend vocabulary – through everyday conversation; using the language of storytelling and acquiring new words connected with topics, themes and play activities
- To show an interest in illustrations of all books and know about title, author and illustrators
- To understand the meaning of fiction and non-fiction
- To explore and identify rhyme in songs, story and everyday activities
- To find and read familiar words in the immediate environment
- To use writing as a means of recording what they see and do and to communicate with others

Permanent resources (changed according to current topic)	Resource provision	Intended experiences (cross-curricular dimensions)	Key vocabulary and questions
Book corner with quality books – dual language; picture; fiction; non-fiction; range of genres of traditional, folk, global and multicultural; multisensory	Adults to stimulate, enthuse and promote an enjoyment and interest in literacy	Children encouraged to listen to and share ideas with peers and adults drawing on experiences from home	Frequent adult support to model and promote language and literacy
Mark-making materials – variety of scribing instruments; paper, envelopes	Adults to listen, share, observe and monitor children's early literacy experiences	Adults and children to make the most of all opportunities to promote language and literacy	**Key vocabulary** Book-handling language – author, title, illustrator, front page, back cover, turn the page, next
Creative materials – paint, chalk, pastels, modelling	Create storying and rhyming through play activities	Children to have access to fiction and non-fiction books related to topics and continuous provision	Encourage rhyming language Promote the structure of stories
Musical instruments and resources to create sounds	Model reading and writing	Make and use clipboards and scribing materials available in activity areas	Share poems, songs and nursery rhymes Promote the 100 high frequency words
Outside – chalking walls; clipboards	Prompt early reading and writing skills, apprenticing children into literacy	Draw children's attention to environmental print	**Key questions** Promote comprehension through varied open and closed questions:
Tape recorders and storybooks; dual-language tapes	Use books, both fiction and non-fiction, at every opportunity	Encourage children to make choices	What do you think happens next? What could happen in the story?
Interactive whiteboard – literacy programmes and stories	Encourage children to use picture cues		Shall we write what we know? Shall we draw a picture?
Jigsaws and language games	Use the interactive whiteboard to promote interactive literacy experiences		

Glossary

Alliteration: where the same sounds appear in the first syllable of two or more consecutive words, e.g. tongue twisters

Bilabial sounds: such as [p], [b], [m] in English where both lips are used as articulators to produce the sound

Bilingualism: fluency in two languages

CGFS: Curriculum Guidance for the Foundation Stage. The curriculum from 2000–2008 for children aged 3 to 5 years

Circle time: a group activity where children sit in a circle, learning more about themselves, each other and communication or emotional literacy skills

Co-construct: when an adult and child are both involved in the learning process and understanding, thinking and meanings are jointly shared

Code switching: when an individual switches between formal and informal language or even between two languages in the course of a conversation

Cohesion: when conversation is fluent

Contextualise: to place a word or idea in context

Conversation: an act of communication between two or more people involving turn-taking, listening and talking

Cuing systems: what readers use to be able to decode/understand the meaning of unknown words in a text, e.g. via semantics, syntax or the grapho-phonemic cues

Deixis: language fixed in the time and place of conversation, such as instructions on where to put things or directions

DfES: Department for Education and Skills. This is now superseded by the Department for Children, Schools and Families, which brings together education and children's services

ELGs: Early Learning Goals

Emergent literacy: initial reading and writing skills that children develop, which lead to them becoming competent readers

Emotional well-being: awareness of one's own emotions; the feel-good factor about oneself that contributes to healthy personal esteem and self-values

Environmental print: words and symbols found in everyday life such as signs, advertisements and product packaging

EPPE: Effective Provision of Preschool Education. A major longitudinal study (1997–2002) that researched the quality of pre-school education in England

EYFS: Early Years Foundation Stage. The new curriculum from birth to age 5 delivered in settings from September 2008

Fine motor skills: movement involving small muscles within the eye or hand, such as in holding a pencil or brush

Gross motor skills: movement involving the larger muscles or whole body, such as walking or lifting the head

High/Scope: the High/Scope curriculum is an approach to education used widely in the USA, specifically designed in the 1960s to improve intellectual performance of children in disadvantaged inner city areas. It is a cognitively-oriented curriculum, based loosely on Piagetion theory with a pedagogy built upon a 'plan-do-review' sequence of activities

Intertextuality: how the meaning of one text is shaped by the meaning of other texts

KEEP: Key Elements in Effective Practice. An evaluation and training tool for local authorities to develop effective practice in early years practitioners

Key worker: the person in the educational setting primarily responsible for particular child/ren

Kinaesthetic: a hands-on approach where people learn from touching, feeling and doing

LAD: language acquisition device

Language delay: when a child is learning language at a slower pace than their peers

LASS: language acquisition support system

Lateralisation: left- or right-handedness

Madrassas: Islamic schools

Metalinguistic awareness: the ability to understand the nature of language, i.e. the structure and systems

Makaton: A system of signs and symbols to teach communication, language and literacy skills to people with communication and learning difficulties. It is an internationally-recognised communication programme, used in more than 40 countries worldwide

Modelling language: being a role model for children in terms of language used

Motherese: adapted or simplified language used by the child's mother in order to communicate with her child or baby

NC: National Curriculum. The official state curriculum that sets out the stages and core subjects children aged 5 to 16 will be taught during their time at school

Ofsted: Office for Standards in Education. The official body for inspecting schools in England

Onomatopoeia: words that convey meaning through sound, e.g. pitter-patter (of rain), crash, bang, swish

Operators: the first words used by babies, which can usually convey a whole range of meanings

Overextension: when a child is applying a wider meaning to the word than is usual in adult language, such as 'car' might refer to all road vehicles or 'cat' to all animals

Paralinguistics: the study of paralanguage, i.e. non-verbal forms of communication such as intonation, pitch and volume, and how they influence meaning

Parentese (or infant directed speech): adapted or simplified language used by the parent, carer, guardian, relative or friend in order to accommodate the understanding of the child or baby

Phoneme: the smallest unit of speech that distinguishes meaning and may be made up of one or more letters that make one sound, e.g. [th], [sch]. There are approximately 44 phonemes in the English language

Phonemic awareness: the ability to distinguish and utilise sounds in a word

Phonetically 'decodable': materials that use only vocabulary and sounds that have been taught to the children

Phonetics: the science of speech sounds

Phonology: the study of the way in which sound is used to express meaning and an analysis of the variations that arise

PNS: Primary National Strategy. The official state strategy that supports teachers and schools to raise standards across the whole curriculum

Playscape: playscapes extend the context of builder's trays, through providing landscapes and environments that can extend children's storytelling and problem solving through contextualising play

Pragmatics: relates to children acquiring the social rules that govern the choice of language in terms of vocabulary, grammar and pronunciation

Pronunciation: the way in which words or sentences are spoken

Scaffolding: assistance provided by an adult in context to aid a child's learning

Schemas: repeated actions or behaviour from experiences that gradually develop into co-ordinated and assimilated activities

Segmentation skills: breaking up a word into its individual sounds, e.g. c–a–t

Semantic learning: the process of understanding concepts and putting vocabulary together to make sense and meaning

Semilingualism: when a child fails to acquire the first language to the same standard as would be anticipated in a monolingual child because first language acquisition is interrupted or insufficient

SEN: special educational needs

SLT: speech and language therapist

Socio-culturalism: how children develop their language, emotional attachments, life expectations and significant relationships in the context of the community in which they are brought up

Special educational needs (SEN): learning difficulties or disabilities that affect a child's ability to learn

Stakeholders: those who have an interest in children's education such as parents, teachers and school governors

Story sack: a large cloth bag which contains a story book and various props to bring the story to life

Storying: occurs as we make up our own stories from anecdotes, personal experiences, written stories, events, culture and history

Sustained shared thinking (SST): sharing intelligent conversations with children and encouraging joint construction of ideas

Syntactic learning: the process of stringing words together to make meaningful sentences

Syntax: the rules or grammar of sentence structure

Telegraphese: when young children omit the small grammatical words such as 'is' or 'are', word endings such as 'ing', or the definite or indefinite article

Timbre: quality and tone of sound

Transliteration: the practice of transcribing a word or text written in one writing system into another writing system

Treasure baskets: a collection of everyday articles that can be used to stimulate a child or baby's senses

Underextension: the limiting of the meaning of a word to the child's own narrow worldview

References

Athey, C. (2007) *Extending Thought in Young Children: A Parent–Teacher Partnership* (2nd edition). London: PCP.

Brock, A. (1999) *Into the Enchanted Forest – Language, Drama and Science in the Primary School*. Stoke-on-Trent: Trentham.

Bryant, P., Bradley, L., Maclean, M. and Crossland, J. (1989) Nursery rhymes, phonological skills and reading. *Journal of Child Language,* 16: 407–428.

Conteh, J. (ed.) (2006) *Promoting Learning for Bilingual Pupils 3–11: Opening Doors to Success*. London: PCP/Sage.

Cooper, H. (2004) *Exploring Time and Place Through Play*. London: David Fulton.

DfES (2005) *KEEP Key Elements of Effective Practice*, London: DfES Publications.

DfES (2007a) *Early Years Foundation Stage*. London: DfES publications.

DfES (2007b) *Letters and Sounds: Principles and Practice of High Quality Phonics*. London: DfES publications.

Fisher, R. and Williams, J. (2004) *Unlocking Creativity: Teaching across the Curriculum*. London: David Fulton.

Fraser, A. (ed.) (1992) *The Pleasure of Reading*. London: Bloomsbury.

Goswami, U. and Bryant, P. (1990) *Phonological Skills and Learning to Read*. Hove: Lawrence Erlbaum.

Gregory, E. (1997) *One Child, Many Worlds: Early Learning in Multicultural Communities*. London: David Fulton.

Jarvis, P. (2006) Rough and tumble play: lessons in life. *Evolutionary Psychology,* 4: 330–346.

Kyratzis, A. (2001) Children's gender indexing in language: from the separate worlds hypothesis to considerations of culture context and power. *Research on Language and Social Interaction*, 34: 1–14.

Language in the National Curriculum (1989) Unpublished project.

Locke, A., Ginsborg, J. and Peers, I. (2002) Development and disadvantage: implications for the early years and beyond. *International Journal of Language and Communication Disorders*, 37 (1): 3–15.

McEvoy, H. and Greer, J. (2007) *What is linguistic phonics?* http://www.belb.org.uk/parents/literacyLinguisticPhonics

Meek, M. (1991) *On Being Literate*. London: Bodley Head.

Mellon, N. (1992) *Storytelling and the Art of Imagination*. Shaftesbury: Element.

NALDIC (National Association for Language Development in the Curriculum) Working Paper 5 (1999) *The distinctiveness of English as an additional language, A cross-curriculum discipline*.

National Centre for Research in Children's Literature (2001) *Evaluation of Bookstart 2001*. Booktrust.

Nutbrown, C. (2006) *Threads of thinking: Young Children Learning*. London: PCP.

Potter, C. (2007) Developments in UK early years policy and practice: can they improve outcomes for disadvantaged children? *International Journal of Early Years Education*, 15 (2): 171–180.

Potter, C. A. and Hodgson, S. (2007) Language enriched preschool settings: a Sure Start training approach, in J. Schneider, M. Avis and P. Leighton (eds), *Supporting Children and Families: Lessons from Sure Start for Evidence-Based Practice*. London: Jessica Kingsley.

Riley, J. (2006) *Language and Literacy 3–7*. London: PCP.

Sage, R. (2006) Supporting language and communication: a guide for school support staff. London: PCP.

Sammons, P., Eliot, K., Sylva, K., Melhuish, E., Siraj-Blatchford, I. and Taggert, P. (2004) The impact of pre-school on young children's cognitive attainments at entry to reception. *British Educational Research Journal*, 30 (5): 692–707.

Siraj-Blatchford, I., Sylva, K., Muttock, S., Gilden, R. and Bell, D. (2002) *Researching Effective Pedagogy in the Early Years*. Research Report 356. London: DfES/Institute of Education, University of London.

Sylva, K. and Pugh, G. (2005) Transforming the early years in England. *Oxford Review of Education*, 31 (1): 11–27.

Sylva, K., Melhuish, E., Sammons, P., Siraj-Blatchford, I. and Taggart, B. (2004) *The Effective Provision of Pre-school Education (EPPE) Project: Final Report*. London: DfES/Institute of Education, University of London.

Vygotsky, L. (1978) *Mind in Society: The Development of Higher Psychological Processes*. Cambridge, MA: MIT Press/Harvard University Press.

Wade, B. and Moore, M. (1998) *A Gift for Life: Bookstart, the First Five Years. A description and evaluation of an exploratory British project to encourage sharing books with babies*. Birmingham: Booktrust.

Weinberger, J., Hannon, P. and Nutbrown, C. (1990) *Ways of Working with Parents to Promote Early Literacy Development*. Sheffield: The University Press of Sheffield/USDE Publications.

Wells, G. (1985) *Language Development in the Pre-School Years*. Cambridge: Cambridge University Press.

Wells, G. (1987) *The Meaning Makers*. Sevenoaks: Hodder & Stoughton.

Welsh Assembly Government (2003) *Iaith Pawb: a National Action Plan for a Bilingual Wales*. Cardiff: WAG.

Whitehead, M. (2004) *Language and Literacy in the Early Years* (3rd edition). London: PCP.

Zimmerman, F. and Christakis, D. (2005) Children's television viewing and cognitive outcomes: a longitudinal analysis of national data. *Archives of Pediatrics and Adolescent Medicine*, 159 (7): 619–625.

Index